ICE COLD AND DEADLY

A True Crime story of one man's redemption and another's destruction

W.M. Korkie

Cover designed by W.M. Korkie

The events described in this book are true. Names have been changed out of respect for the victims. Any resemblance to other persons, living or dead, events, or locales is entirely coincidental.

CONTENTS

CHAPTER 1 – VOID

I cut through the water feeling the sensation of my previously sweaty body cooling, and at the same time, relaxing. It's hot out, and I need to cool my skin from the California sun. As I come up for air and wipe the chlorinated water out of my eyes, Sherwood looks at me from beside the pool with his quizzical look. His eyes narrow as his ears tweak forward, and I imagine that he's probably thinking, *Why are you in the water*? Typically, any time there's water around, I'm the one admonishing *him* to either stay or get out of the water, depending on the situation.

Suddenly, Sherwood's expression changes from quizzical to cautious: his body tenses and his ears move back flat on his head. He fails to realize quickly enough that I have inched my way closer, to edge of the pool. Close enough to slap my hand across the pool in his direction and send an arc of water pouring over him. Tail between his legs, he scurries to safety a good twenty feet away. How can a 90-pound Labrador retriever mix with webbed paws be bothered by a few drops of water that quickly run off his bristly, golden fur? I don't feel sorry for him. I also don't feel bad that Chico got caught in the splash. Chico is the annoying little Chihuahua mix that has fallen in love with Sherwood's leg.

Sherwood and I have been together for nine and a half years and have experienced several challenging life situations, but now we're living the high life. It's July, I'm temporarily unemployed and we have the run of a beautiful home with a swimming pool on the edge of Beverly Hills. Sherwood has plenty of other dogs to play with, and he's the boss. This is fortunate because he is a strong alpha, who is perfectly willing to take on all comers.

The other five dogs living in the Bercham home with us include eleven-year-old Snicker, who likes to hang out in my bedroom; Munchkin, the crippled poodle mix; Pablo, another Chihuahua; Maxi the chow, and Pumpkin. Pumpkin is my first clue that Graeme has a weakness for flawed, insufferable women. She's his favorite, and is also the most obnoxious little bitch of a dog I've ever met. The first time I tried to pet her, she tolerated it for about two seconds, then slowly curled her lip, and tried to bite my hand. Graeme made a weak attempt at scolding her but she seemed to know that nothing was going to happen. Even a dog can sense that high-maintenance females rule Graeme Bercham's existence.

I look around the large backyard to see who is outside with us. It's just Sherwood and the leg humper. With seven dogs around, it's hard to keep their shit off my shoes, but Graeme's gardeners come often enough that the place looks great. The palms that surround the pool have been recently manicured, and the brick work of the fire pit is freshly re-mortared. It is a pleasant environment that shrouds a lurking danger. I have just finished tearing out the ugly, wooden handicap ramp that led up to the sliding glass doors. It is no longer needed because of the suspicious death of the person it was built for, and she won't be the last person to die here.

Past the hot tub at the end of the swimming pool, there's a trellised area with deck furniture. Graeme and I have our hockey equipment drying out on the chairs after a good skate at Culver City Ice Arena. We share a love of hockey that so many northerners do—it was how we met. Most Canadian males, me included, see hockey as our birthright, and Minnesotans are not so different. Graeme left there thirty years ago to attend law school and eventually raise his family in L.A., but he never forgot about hockey. He was into hockey in California long before hockey was cool in California. Around the house, there are the pictures of him coaching his two sons in the early 80's, the pre-Wayne Gretzky era.

When we sit on the bench at Culver, Graeme loves to tell stories about California hockey. Like the time he played with Mike Myers—well, actually, nobody could really play because Mike spent the whole session cracking jokes. Or about Tim Robbins who also played at Culver occasionally and has the reputation around there of being an arrogant ass. Another one about how his son, Grant, had an absolute cannon of a shot but none of the intestinal fortitude required to excel. My favorite was the time he recognized Gretzky at the grocery store in the days following his trade from Edmonton. Apparently, Wayne's life had been so tumultuous that he hadn't had the time to set up any of his banking. Being Wayne Gretzky in Edmonton would probably get you the benefit of the doubt if you were short of money in the grocery line, but not in L.A. circa September 1988. Not unless California Hockey Fan # 1 happened to be standing behind you. On at least three separate occasions, I've heard from Graeme how he paid for Wayne's groceries, told him what a huge fan he was, and welcomed him to L.A. I've chosen to believe the story, but even if it isn't true I still love it. You see, I lived the Gretzky trade from the other side of the transaction. Wayne was ripped out of our city as the world changed on us, and we were being left behind. Now, seventeen years later, I'm living in L.A. and associating with people who have interacted with him in his new life. I feel like some of the lost connection has been regained.

Hockey is in my blood, having played it since I was five years old. Even though I'm 36 now, and have given up the game for three years in favor of golf, I can still stand out in a pickup game. Graeme is always looking to improve his team, so it only took a couple of sessions for him to invite me to play for his "A" division team. At 56, Graeme is by no means an "A" division player, but he runs the team, so who can argue with that? And in spite of Graeme's weakness as a player, I've come to realize what an important part of the team he really is. In addition to the Monday night "A" league, Graeme and I play three times a week. We've become fast friends: he wants good players on his team, I appreciate his generosity and lifestyle, and we share the passion for hockey.

I climb out of the water, walk over to the lounge chair and sit down. There isn't a cloud in the sky and I feel great, even experience a short burst of euphoria. Then, as always, the pain washes over me—it's never far away these days. I've lived with depression for most of my life, but the last couple of years have been the worst of my life.

* * *

Back in September 2004, almost two years ago, I graduated with an MBA from the University of North Carolina. My parents came down to Chapel Hill from Stony Plain, Alberta to be with my wife Sandra and me and our 4 year-old twins. Going back to school at the age of 32 with a job, a business, and a family had been a challenging undertaking, and successfully completing the degree made me feel as though I could achieve whatever I wanted. But my graduation was a high point that I would not reach again for a long time.

My downward spiral started in school when I developed a business idea for a men's fitness system. It had always been a dream of mine to own a sports-related business, and with this new idea I felt I had something special. A computer programmer by trade, I developed an automated workout system that I was certain was better than anything available. Sandra and I had already opened Raleigh's first Curves franchise two years earlier and were rewarded financially. So armed with a business plan, and presumably the support of my wife, I opened Second Wind Circuit Training on December 16, 2004. On December 31, Sandra informed me that she wanted a divorce.

She had given me two weeks to pursue my dream.

I can't say Sandra's decision was a complete surprise because we were never really happy together. Still, the timing of her decision was like an aggressive knife to the back. Added to the pain was that we continued to live together in our house for the first three months of 2005, and then she told me that she wanted me out of our house by the end of March. To this day, I still wonder why I agreed to move out of our 3500 sq ft house instead of asking her to leave. I had earned, by far, the lion's share of the income over the course of our marriage and felt that I had as many rights to the children as she did. Perhaps it was out of fear that she would take me to court, go live with the children and her parents in South Dakota, and then ruin our already shaky finances battling over the assets. Or maybe it was because I didn't want Sandra to make my addiction problems public thereby guaranteeing that my fitness business would fail. But most likely, it was because I thought it was better if I focused on my business given the vulnerable phase it was in. As it was, I did agree to move out, and in April, my parents came down again — this time to help me get settled in my new 700 sq ft apartment.

Second Wind grew for the first half of 2005, and was even featured in an article in the *Raleigh News & Observer*. Ironically, the reporter wanted to focus on the husband and wife angle. Since we were technically still married and were jointly operating the businesses, we went along with the story. The publicity caused a brief membership boon, but it was fleeting.

By the end of the year, despite my efforts and thousands of dollars in marketing, it was clear that Second Wind was not going to support me. The financial pressure of the divorce meant that I would have had to borrow a good deal of money for the chance that it might take off. I kept it open into 2006 while I looked for a job, but I was having no more success finding a job than I was running a business. Even with an MBA from a respected school and over ten years of corporate experience, it seemed that employers equated my self-employment with unemployment.

Meanwhile, in August, Sandra had decided that it was time to get involved with another man, which put my self-esteem at an all-time low. A stagnant business, a soon-to-be ex-wife introducing a new man into my children's life, and limited job prospects were all too much for me to handle. On April 14, 2006, I moved 2500 miles away from my children to Stony Plain, broken. The day before I left, Sandra served me with the final summons for the divorce. I had no other option than to leave Raleigh and go back to live with my parents.

I kept wondering how it could happen that after earning the living for my family I was so completely devastated financially by the divorce. Granted, I had made the risky decision to start a new business, but I also took steps to mitigate. Two years earlier, I borrowed the Curves startup money from my parents and worked together with Sandra to build a solid franchise operation. I also started Second Wind in a way that it wouldn't require large capital expenditures and would start covering its variable costs quickly. In spite of my efforts, I hadn't come close to eliminating the risk. Risk-Reward sounds straightforward enough—the greater the risk the greater the chance you have for high a return, but I have lived the dark side of risk. Do not underestimate the lows that you can hit if you are not properly prepared for failure. My mother often said, "Better to aim for the stars and hit the fence than to aim for the fence and hit the dust."

Nice thought, but if you stay firmly planted on the ground, you don't bang into anything. When I shut my business down, I felt as though I had spent the previous ten years going backward banging into things the whole way. All I could think about was the wasted time, money, and effort I had poured into my dream. I was too selfish to focus on the two amazing kids who adored me. Instead, I frequently obsessed about the six-figure income I had earned for many years that was now all gone. And because I was having trouble finding a job, the human capital I'd accumulated meant nothing to me. I had worked countless hours fixing up our houses in an effort to build equity, and I didn't think the profit from the sale of our current home was anywhere near commensurate with my effort. It seemed like I'd be starting over again, and I simply couldn't conceive of that.

The first couple weeks in the dust of Alberta were exactly what I needed. My parents took care of me as best they could, and I let them. It was comforting to know that I could stay there as long as I wanted. My zest for life was gone, and I had no plans to ever move out of their home. I worked with Dad around the house a little bit, ran eight miles a day, caught up with hometown friends that I usually got to see only once a year, and for the first time in my adult life, I spent an extended period of time with my parents without tension. I didn't have the stress of running interference between my wife and parents, who never really got along. I didn't have to justify my parenting methods to anybody. Nor did I have to try and earn a living to keep up with my wife's propensity for spending money. I was able to just relax and not feel pressure from anything or anyone. My parents saved my life.

For a month, the break from the deluge of life continued. After that, I started to get restless, and I think the first step of my long journey back to health was that I regained my pride. I realized again that I have too many skills to warrant sponging off my parents. The turning point came one evening when we watched *Failure to Launch*. The movie is certainly not Matthew McConaughey's best effort, but it resonated for me. I was a traumatized 36-year-old living with his parents watching a movie about the exact same situation. My dad watched about twenty minutes and then left the room. I'm not sure if it was because the movie was so bad or because he saw the parallel too. Whatever the case, the movie made me feel extremely uneasy, and jarred something in me—finally I felt motivated again. Within a month, it was time to leave the nest again, so I chose Los Angeles for a fresh start.

* * *

Now, three months later, I've managed to derail myself again. I had been working for Disney but quit within a month. Disney is notorious for being cheap and treating its employees poorly, but I had taken the job anyway. I wrongly assumed that having a manager designation would mitigate some of the downside. My role was that of marketing manager, which was relatively new for me, and their technical infrastructure was terrible. To make matters worse, I was finding out that my real title was actually *Manager of Cut and Paste Operations*.

In addition to the normal job stress, my fuse was extra short because of the drugs. I found huge bottles of Valium containing as many as 500 pills in one of Graeme's cupboards, so I took some for myself. Through lecture, experimentation, and reading, I have learned about the pendulum effect of drugs.

Whatever effects the drug has when it's in your system, the opposite effects will be magnified when it leaves your system. I was taking Valium at nights to calm down, so during the day I was edgy and irritable. My tenure at this impossible job at Disney came to an end when I was told that several extremely tedious, entry-level tasks were a regular part of the job description. Even with the clearest of minds, I may have felt that the position had been misrepresented and given two weeks notice, but in my state I quit on the spot. It likely would have been better to tough it out for a while, but my behavior is still erratic at times.

In any case, unemployment feels pretty good when I'm sitting by a pool on a perfect Los Angeles day. I'm living for free with Graeme as I had been with my parents, but the situation doesn't seem as bleak. I've proven to myself that I can land a job in Corporate America, and I've impressed a perfect stranger with my personality and hockey skills. Beyond that, Graeme's motivations are not clear: he may be extending his friendship because he suspects that I've been through an extremely difficult time and he is an altruistic soul. Or, more likely, it's because he has created an emptiness in his life that he needs to fill.

CHAPTER 2 – THE UNFORTUNATE SON

I met Graeme on my second day in L.A, and two weeks later, he invited me to a BBQ at his house. I was excited to see it because I had already heard a lot about how nice it was. The evening was promising—lots of fun and single people there, and Graeme told me to bring along anyone I wanted. I decided to bring my friend George, whom I'd been staying with since arriving in L.A. In fact, George was the one who initially convinced me that L.A. was worth checking out. He had recently started working as a computer consultant to a major investment company, and there were recruiters calling him every day. He offered to let me stay at his place while I investigated the job market for financial analysts. While job hunting, I was also scoping the social situation. We had gone out to various L.A. landmark bars like the Rainbow Room and the Whiskey, but after nine years of marriage the club scene had little appeal. I was looking for more laidback settings where image is less important than wit. Graeme's party sounded perfect.

We showed up at his house fairly early, but Graeme was already half in the bag. He introduced us to his assistant Lindsay and her boyfriend Patrick. They were in charge of the refreshments and were busily cooking. His lifestyle enticed me immediately. He was throwing a party, enjoying himself, and Lindsay was taking care of all the busywork. Then we got the tour of his home, which was equally impressive. It had all the indications of wealth—leather furniture, antique wood tables, large screen televisions and an impressive display of art. Any painting that wasn't an original was a rare print. He told me the names of the artists, but it was all lost on me because I don't follow art. I did find that the pieces were pleasant to look at, and recognized that everything had been put together with a purpose. This, I thought, was the kind of house I'd love to live in. I had spent the last few weeks getting familiar with the L.A. apartment rental market and the sticker shock that went along with it, so I was starting to do the math on what it would cost to live in such a home.

By the time he was done showing us around, the other guests were starting to arrive. One of the first was Graeme's son Grant—although Grant wasn't technically a guest. He had been living in the house since his mother, Julia, passed away at the beginning of the year. Then when Graeme moved back into the house, it was time for him to find a place of his own. When he got there, we were standing in the kitchen chatting.

Graeme turned to him, "This is Mike."

He must have mentioned me to Grant because there was a look of recognition on his face. I felt a bit uneasy that Graeme was already talking to his son about me because I really hadn't known him that long. Grant had a very gregarious manner about him and as we shook hands he said, "I'm Grant, Graeme's unfortunate son."

Delivered with a nasally drone, the comment was both humorous and disarming—and also true. Months later, it would turn out to be the most ironic thing that anyone has ever said to me.

While touring the house, I had noticed a picture of Grant as a young adult. He was extremely good looking, the type of guy that most women would be attracted to. The man that stood in front of me was not. There were some obvious, drastic changes – he had seemingly aged about twenty years. The younger Grant had an attractive head of short, curly blondish hair; this Grant had shaved his head to a five o'clock shadow. Younger Grant wasn't muscular, but had a good physique nonetheless; this Grant wasn't fat but had grown flabby as if he hadn't exercised from the time the picture was taken. This Grant had also covered most of his arms and neck with tattoos, was a chain smoker and had an overly relaxed body language suggesting that he was high on opiates. Then, he introduced his fiancée, Lindsay, a woman the young Grant likely wouldn't have looked at twice. She was less than physically appealing—she was also chain smoking cigarettes and her eyes had the gray, filmy look of someone who has damaged her body time and again. Most notable was her demeanor: it said to me that life had completely defeated her. Grant and his fiancée were the first noticeable hint that Graeme's life was far from perfect.

After some small talk, Graeme and I separated ourselves from Grant and went out poolside to meet some of the other guests. Stephanie, the current love of Graeme's life, had arrived. She was an extremely beautiful woman, a former actress who had just been accepted as a graduate student into the UCLA biology department. I was impressed because I could actually find her on imdb.com, which is the best online database of information related to movies, actors, television shows. Her roommate, also named George, worked in the entertainment industry screening movies for the purpose of gauging audience responses before final edit. He began telling stories about celebrities he had worked with like Jim Carrey and Vince Vaughn. I spent a good part of the afternoon by the pool talking to him about his star-studded experiences.

Graeme had fallen in unrequited love with Stephanie while his wife was still alive. Technically, Graeme was a widower, but his marriage had been complicated at best. He and Julia had been legally separated for many years and dated other people. He explained that it made sense not to divorce because of legal issues surrounding the property they owned together. I don't really buy that explanation; I'm more inclined to see them as codependent. Graeme had asked Stephanie to marry him but told her not to answer immediately, likely because he knew that her answer would be no. But if she ever changed her mind, he wanted her to know that he was available. While he waited for her to say yes, he did things for her, and she let him. He helped her study for, and pass, her graduate admissions tests. Every week he took her out to a platonic dinner hoping that would be the day she changed her mind. For completing her bachelor degree, he bought her a $3000 computer system. He had it in his office to give it to her at the party, but it needed some configuration. My friend George offered to set it up for her. Graeme accepted, so while I was outside they went inside to work on the computer. By *work on,* I mean George tinkered, and Graeme drank.

I knew that Graeme was well-off, but I still thought it was ridiculous to spend that much money on a woman who wasn't committed to him. It was obvious that he was buying the computer as a yet another enticement for her to date him. He apparently refused to accept that she had already decided, but then Graeme wasn't a realist. The first time I went out to the bar with the hockey team, he made a revealing statement. We were sitting around talking when he suddenly announced, "I may be older, but you young guys have no money! Women like guys with money."

His comment was not only unsolicited but also out of place within the conversation. Graeme was insecure and desperate for female attention; in other words, he was an easy target.

Someone whom women could not manipulate was Graeme's other son Ryan. He showed up at the house about halfway into the party, and while he was nothing like Grant, my first impression of him was also negative. Ryan seemed put off that his dad was having a party, so he basically just stormed through the house, did something in the backroom, and left. Graeme was quick to tell me that Ryan was gay, as though that were an excuse for his petulant behavior. He also told me that Ryan was a law student at Loyola Marymount, which turned out to be a half-truth because he was actually a philosophy major. Perhaps he planned on going to law school after he graduated, but there is a big difference between planning on and actually doing. I suspect that the law student story was merely wishful thinking by Graeme, a way for a wannabe alpha male to be able to relate to his gay son.

I was enjoying myself, but it was a pool party and so far no single women. George was still inside nerding with the computer when Sarah showed up. Graeme's assistant Lindsay invited not only her boyfriend but also her best friend Sarah. She was 23 years old, sexy and, most important, single. She spent the first fifteen minutes talking with Lindsay and Patrick, so I didn't really have a chance to meet her. As I was talking to Stephanie and George, I was also looking for an opportunity to break away and talk to Sarah. Before I had the chance to, however, she approached the table and sat down beside me – must have been because I was wearing my lucky blue shirt. I deliberately bought it a size too small ascribing to the belief that if you want big muscles, wear a tight shirt. She introduced herself, and we hit it off right away.

We talked for about twenty minutes, and I was on my game. Her body language was open, and she touched her hair several times. Even though I am typically clueless about women, I picked up on her flirting. Since I was very new to L.A., we were talking a lot about life in Southern California. She stated that she thought most of the local guys were shallow, and they all had gimmicks. I told her that my gimmick was sincerity. She laughed and touched my arm. I thought, *this chick likes you*; don't screw it up.

We chatted for a while longer before Lindsay wanted Sarah to help her with something, so I decided to go back inside and see what Graeme was up to. By this time he was obviously drunk but still coherent. Graeme knew that I was still sleeping on George's air mattress, and he asked me how my apartment hunting was progressing. It had been a very difficult process because it's hard to find an apartment in L.A. when you have a big dog. I felt a sense of urgency about getting a place because I had just accepted the position with Disney. I told Graeme about the guesthouse in Burbank that I had decided to rent.

He said, "Oh, that's too bad."

"Why?"

"Because I have a proposition for you. You could move in with me and help me with things that I need done around here." He then explained that I could work about 30 hours per month for him on projects around his house in lieu of rent. Since, I was in debt and trying to get back on my feet, the deal sounded incredible. There was also no comparison between Graeme's house and the guesthouse. I considered for a moment whether or not I was willing to do the daily hour-long commute from Beverlywood to Glendale. It didn't take long for me to decide that the offer was too good to pass up, but then another problem occurred to me. Would Sherwood get along with the rest of the pack?

We agreed that I should go and get him right then to see how he would respond. At about this time, Sarah and Lindsay decided it was time to go swimming. I really wanted to stay and check that out, but I was thinking big picture. Besides it had only taken me about fifteen minutes to get there, so I figured that I would be back fairly quickly.

Goddamned L.A traffic. I had been struggling to figure out the on/off ramps ever since I arrived. When you miss an interchange in this city, it's at least a five-minute mistake. Apparently, the sadistic city planners had decided long ago that symmetry is boring and no two interchanges would be the same. The paranoid Canadian in me imagined that one of these times I was going to take a wrong turn straight into a gang-infested hellhole. On my way back to George's apartment, I missed at least three interchanges, and traffic was significantly worse than when I went to the party. An hour later I got back to the house with Sherwood and found out that Sarah was leaving for another party. *Fuck.* As she left, she came over and gave me a big hug and said, "We should do something like this again." *Score.*

Now I needed to turn my attention to the chaos that was the dog situation. Graeme was currently fully blitzed and had a nasty cut on his head. While I was trying to navigate the insane

L.A. road system, Graeme was having just as much trouble trying to navigate the fire pit in his back yard. He was not going to be much help with the dogs, so introducing them one at a time would take forever. I decided I would just let Sherwood into the yard and hope for the best. Of course Sherwood and Maxi fought almost immediately, and I thought that my opportunity was ruined. Luckily, Graeme didn't freak out, and when I pulled Sherwood off of her everything was fine. With the dog situation settled, I now had a place to stay. I was going to be working at Disney, I would be living in a beautiful home, and I had met a new friend, Sarah. For the first time in over a year, things were looking up.

Before long, everybody left the party except for George, James and his girlfriend Emily, and me. James was another hockey player I had met at Culver City, and we bonded very quickly. We were both good players born in Saskatchewan, and what more do two guys need to become friends? It was only late afternoon, so we sat in the hot tub talking about our mutual friend, who we hoped had passed out from the alcohol not a concussion. I already knew that Graeme liked to imbibe, but this party had shown me just how much. George told us how Graeme had managed to hit his head. We laughed a little bit, but mostly felt sorry for him. I also told them about my new living situation, and I was surprised at James' reaction.

"Watch out for Graeme," he said.

It was a provocative statement, and I needed to know more, "What do you mean? Is he dangerous or something?"

"No, he's just a little weird. It's hard to explain, I just kind of have a feeling about him."

I find it irritating when people pique my interest and then don't elaborate, but at that time James knew Graeme much better than he knew me. I respected that he didn't want to bad mouth his friend and thought it was nice that he was willing to share some insight about my new roommate. Other than his sons, and perhaps some excessive drinking, I hadn't noticed anything too disturbing about Graeme. What I saw at that point was a high living, successful businessman with lots of friends.

The next day, I spoke with Graeme, and I was a little nervous about bringing up our agreement. After all, he had been drunk enough to pass out, so he might not even remember making it. I was relieved when he told me he remembered the discussion but had forgotten the terms. I reminded him what they were, and he was still fine with them. So, in spite of James' vague warning, I was excited to move in.

CHAPTER 3 – ROOMMATES

I had to wait a few days to move into the house because Grant was finishing moving out, and I was getting his room. Job one was cleaning my new bedroom and adjacent bathroom. Apparently, Graeme's weekly maid service didn't extend to Grant's wing because it looked like it hadn't been fully cleaned in over a year. If the dried urine in the bathroom wasn't enough to piss me off, there were also cigarette butts strewn all over the place. It was a hovel within a mansion, but over the course of a few days, I got the mess cleaned and the room became mine.

Part of the clean-up job had been helping Graeme empty Julia's things out of my room. If my closet was any indication, Julia's whole house must have been a medicine chest. While Graeme was holding back tears and trying to decide which outfits to hold onto and which to trash, I was about to explode trying not to ask some obvious questions. *What the hell is Ciprofloxacin? Why are there several cases of it gathering dust in the closet? What were all these inhalers for, and why did she need so many?* The ones in my closet were obviously spares.

I certainly couldn't ask these questions of the emotional man standing next to me without feeling like a complete asshole. When I was able to get to the Internet I found out that Cipro was primarily used to fight infections but could also be used to treat anthrax poisoning. This information only brought to mind more questions. Had she stockpiled it for some paranoid fear of an Anthrax attack? Did she die of AIDS? Cancer? Graeme obviously saw the same things in the closet that I did and would have known the answers to my questions, but he wasn't volunteering any information.

I decided not to risk pissing off my charitable landlord for information that I would probably get eventually anyway. I needed Graeme's generosity right then. Although I had started working as a marketing analyst for Disney, I wasn't 100% sure that it would last, and I had no savings. I calculated that my morbid curiosity would probably not be an endearing quality, so I kept it to myself.

Once the cleaning was finished, the next order of business was to replace my borrowed air mattress with a real bed. Sandra had been nice enough to keep the king-sized mattress and hand-made, aspen frame for herself. Our guest bed was ten years old, and I had decided that it would not make the cross-country trip from North Carolina. No problem, I had Graeme's hockey network to tap into. While sitting on the bench at Culver pickup, Graeme introduced me to Jeff the mattress guy. His prices were wholesale (retail is for suckers), and two days later my new bed was delivered and set up for me in my room.

I was glad to get my bed up off of the floor because seven indoor dogs can get a little annoying at bedtime. All the dogs had free access to my air mat, and I felt that it was going to be difficult to maintain activity in the bed if there was dog hair all over it. Fortunately, Pumpkin and Munchkin were always in Graeme's room, and Maxi was a loner. Sherwood and Snicker were always in my room, but the new bed was too far off of the ground for them. Unfortunately, two Mexicans thwarted my plan for a hair-free bed. Pablo and Chico were rovers, finding a comfortable sleep wherever they could, and they had no problem sneaking up onto my bed.

Many nights I would wake up with a start, certain that there was a snake or a rat attacking my feet. That's how my dreaming mind translated a Chihuahua jumping up, climbing under the duvet, and curling up in my feet. Some people might like that type of thing, but it freaked me out and they got the boot. A couple of months later, all dogs were banned from Graeme's room, and my room became even more crowded.

With the living/sleeping arrangements set, it was time to start earning my stay. The first task that Graeme assigned me was to accompany him and Lindsay to one of his storage spaces. This wasn't a budget self-storage place, but instead, an expensive, high security place where Graeme stored much of his art collection. As we drove east down I-10 from the house to the storage unit, Graeme mentioned that Grant would be meeting us at the storage unit to help. Lindsay immediately made a negative comment and asked whether it was really a good idea. I was curious as to what the problem would be with having another set of hands to get things done.

When we got there, I quickly found out—Grant has the impulse filter of a five-year-old. He must have pleaded, "Can I have this?" fifteen times. Graeme could hardly concentrate on the task at hand, which was to catalogue all the artwork and other collectables stuffed into his unit. Like every other storage space, garage, or closet that Graeme owned, this unit was packed to the rafters. Getting to one item meant moving at least four others. We were taking pictures of specific pieces that were going to be put up for auction, so the sorting process was not trivial. Once we had an item that he wanted to photograph, we carefully transported it to the specially lit room provided for just this purpose. The process took about three hours because there were well over 100 paintings, thousands of baseball and hockey cards, and drawers full of jewelry and other valuables. Grant took particular interest in a $5000 ring that had belonged to his mother. He and Graeme argued for at least ten minutes about whether Grant should get the ring. I had never seen a 27-year-old man shamelessly whine in front of a relative stranger. Clearly, getting what he wanted meant a lot more to him than my perception of his behavior.

Finally, Grant gave up arguing, the ring got put back, and the issue was supposedly resolved. Unfortunately it was not. Grant had quit harassing his father only because he'd formulated a plan. While we were off taking pictures and cataloguing other items, Grant took the ring. Within days, he had hawked it for pennies on the dollar. When Graeme found out about that a couple of weeks later, he was livid, but he did nothing because he knew that it would be like trying to get blood from a stone. In Grant's mind, he was entitled to the ring, and there was nothing anybody was going to do to stop him from getting it. I was getting first-hand exposure to a dysfunctional child of financial privilege.

I can see now that Graeme Bercham is the worst enabler I have ever met. At that time, however, I was not willing to judge him too harshly because I felt sorry for him having to deal with such a complete loser of a son. I also had sympathy for him because of his distress over his other son, Ryan. It's obvious to me that he can't accept having a gay son. To his credit, Graeme never says a bad word about that part of Ryan's identity, and compared to Grant, Ryan is a dream. He seems responsible and intelligent, and he never presses Graeme's buttons the way Grant does. Occasionally, I hear Graeme on the phone arguing with Ryan, but the conversations typically end with, "OK. I love you. Talk to you later."

On the other hand, phone conversations with Grant involve a lot of yelling. Graeme tries the tough-love approach and tells him not to call until he gets a job. Grant doesn't need a job, but Graeme wants him to get one just for the structure and responsibility. I assume that Grant gets defensive and gives all sorts of reasons that he can't work because those conversations end with Graeme hanging up on him. No *I love you* for Grant, just a frustrated father showing his disgust for his son's behaviors by cutting him off.

Graeme has confided to me that Ryan has had a chip on his shoulder because of an annuity Grant received when he turned eighteen. As a baby, he suffered injuries caused by a fall from a faulty high chair, and Graeme negotiated a significant settlement from the manufacturer. The income disparity contributed to a rebellious period for Ryan, but he moved past it and is working hard in school. He is taking his life in a positive direction, and Graeme empathizes with him, which adds to

Graeme's intolerance of Grant's laziness. Just the other day, we were standing in the driveway as Grant backed his BMW over a shrub and nearly into us. Graeme's eyes nearly popped out of his head, and he made a move like he was going jump on the hood and smash through the window like the zombie from the beginning of Dawn of the Dead. Instead, he just yelled, "You fuckin' asshole!"

Yes, Grant Bercham is a lazy asshole, but from my perspective, his indifference towards life is actually helpful. Grant doesn't appear to care one way or the other if I live with his father rent-free. Conversely, Ryan is a voice of suspicion. When he found out I was moving into the house, he asked Graeme, "Who is this guy, and what do you know about him?"

Graeme put Ryan at ease by telling him that I was Canadian.

"Oh, OK then."

And that was it. Ryan's suspicion of me immediately lessened. I didn't understand how simply being Canadian could absolve me of suspicion. I have since found out that before Ryan went through his 12-step program he had a meth-using boyfriend in the Maritimes. They are still friendly, hence the positive image of Canadians.

It is apparent now that Graeme is not living exactly the charmed life I had initially thought. I've known him for only a month and have already observed significant family dysfunction.

I don't think that Ryan has ever served prison time as Grant has, but both sons seem to have been natured and/or nurtured into self-destructive behavior. Many people might look down their noses at Graeme and his family because of the way they live. Thinking that they deserve whatever misery they get is easy, unless you consider how quickly our human imperfections can ruin us.

I have watched the *Dateline – To Catch A Predator* series, which is essentially a televised Internet sting operation. Adult men are led to believe that they are communicating with a young boy or girl, and invariably, the conversations turn sexual. The men are invited to meet the decoy at a normal-looking middle-class home. Like dogs drawn to a bitch in heat, they show up from hundreds of miles around. Instead of meeting their *date*, they meet Chris Hansen who attempts to interview them inside the house. When they ask if they can go, he tells them that they are free to leave, but they are arrested as soon as they step outside. In most states, it is a felony to even talk to a minor, or even someone you believe to be a minor, about the possibility of a lewd act.

I can't help but find myself hoping that the predators find some way to get out of their predicament. A small part of my reason for this is that I've always cheered for the underdog, the situation isn't real, and no one was ever really going to get hurt.

The main reason, though, is that I understand that these men are about to have their lives destroyed by their weaknesses. The magnitude of their crimes makes me cringe, and I am saddened by the harm to those around them.

Almost all these criminals have people in their life who will be devastated by their actions. Some will have children, who will try to comprehend as their father tries to explain to them that he won't be around for a long time. Entire families will suffer the consequence of seeing their loved-one only during visiting hours. Obviously, sexual predators have no place in our society, and I am glad that they are routinely given five year sentences. In fact, most of these men have so little control over themselves that they are generally beyond rehabilitation, but I empathize with them. In my darkest hours, my lack of self-control harmed my children, parents, and brothers.

I find it frightening how quickly we can go from being a contributing member of society to incarcerated criminal. We have so many laws, with so much gray area, that there are literally thousands of ways to get sent to prison. It is arrogant to think that it cannot happen to you because even driving a car puts you at risk. Almost everybody at some point has had a drink or two and then driven home. Those who make that mistake and then kill somebody in an accident will serve a lengthy prison sentence. One need not even be impaired to be charged and convicted of vehicular manslaughter. Simply driving recklessly or angrily can have the same result. A Colorado man was convicted of first-degree murder for slamming his brakes in front of another car during a fit of road rage.

Even exercising constitutionally protected rights can land you in prison for the rest of your life. Millions of law abiding citizens are staunch defenders of the 2nd Amendment and carry a firearm for self-defense. How many of those people have gotten into an altercation that either got physical or threatened to? If you ever plan to use a weapon to defend yourself, you had better be absolutely certain that a jury of your peers would consider your actions to be justifiable. If they don't, self-defense becomes murder.

CHAPTER 4 – TWO MINUTES FOR HOOKING

It's early July and our Culver "A" team is coming together. Playoffs aren't for another two months, but Graeme is getting excited. His favorite place to talk hockey is the Beverly Wilshire Hotel. We usually go on Wednesday evenings, drink at the corner of the bar, and discuss team strategy. There are a couple of nice lounges, and it's a relaxed place to connect with interesting people. Stephanie is still not interested in him romantically, so if we happen to meet women there, even better. Graeme has developed a Friar Tuck haircut and a Buddha belly, so he generally breaks the ice with women by asking them what they think of me. I find this uncomfortable, and even though this ploy gets all of us into a conversation, I'm not always in the mood for it. Occasionally, he gets irritated with me for not being more interactive and once commented, "You've got the looks, but sometimes you can be downright pouty."

It is true that I have little tolerance for small talk. Conversely, Graeme seems to love starting up conversations with complete strangers, and he is always optimistic about his chances.

"Where have you been all my life?" he half-jokingly says as he pulls a plastic baggie containing his beloved blue pill from his jacket. He is constantly extolling the virtues of Viagra, but I'm not sure when he would have the chance to use it productively.

This night, his efforts pay off, sort of. We're sitting in our usual spot, with an empty chair between us because the place is nearly deserted. A young, blond girl walks over and sits down at the bar by herself. I don't find her particularly attractive—about a six – but Graeme goes right into his routine. He invites her to come sit with us, and she quickly responds by sliding into the chair next to him. He introduces himself and starts his usual bullshit about how great our hockey team is. She cuts him off immediately and tells him that she isn't into talking. He catches on right away, seems intrigued, and they immediately start speaking in hushed tones. The only audible words of the rest of the conversation are Graeme saying, "Oh, so we're negotiating now."

I'm a bit uncomfortable, so I keep my attention focused elsewhere. I notice that the bartenders, whom Graeme knows well, are doing their best impression of Secret Servicemen. This happens to be the hotel in which Pretty Woman was filmed, so I doubt that this is the first time for this type of business transaction to take place here. In the movie, the hotel manager tells Julia Roberts' character that he knows what she is and that she's not welcome. In real life, there are hookers here every night, it's obvious who they are, and nobody bothers them.

Graeme's negotiations are completed in less than five minutes. They get up from the bar together.

"I'll call in a little while," he says as he gives me his keys. He also makes a point of taking his pill as he is leaving. Thanks for that little bit of theater Graeme. Discretion is never on his list of priorities, and I'm sure that I'm not the only person who sees him take it.

"Let's go Graeme," the woman doesn't want him chit-chatting now that they're on the clock.

I figure it's about time Graeme gets some return on his investment. Stephanie and others are just using him for his money; he may as well get something out of it too. He is a lonely, horny guy whose dead wife apparently told him he was a terrible lover. I think he spends a lot of time trying to prove her wrong – as if she's taking notice from the afterlife!

It is fairly late when they leave, and the lounge is basically empty. I want to go home, but I know Graeme wouldn't leave me stranded. I have also just moved in with him and don't want to sour the situation. I speak with Graeme's favorite bartender for a while, and he acts as though he has seen nothing. After about an hour, I'm the last person in the bar and about to be kicked out. I try calling Graeme, but of course there is no answer, so I decided to go out to his car and wait there for another half hour. Finally, he calls and gives me directions. I drive to the corner where he says he'll be and can't help but notice how nice the area is. I'd love to see where the really good-looking hookers conduct their business.

Graeme gets in the passenger seat, and I drive away. I don't want to but feel obligated to ask, "So?"

"It was ok...all very mechanical...I'm not sure I would do that again."

"Well what did you think; she was going to fall in love with you? Of course, it was mechanical," I say.

"I guess you're right. Do me a favor, don't tell the guys." He is embarrassed, and I can tell that this is a first for him.

"I won't. I'll just tell them that you hooked up." He seems to be relieved about that, and I'm relieved not to be getting any more details.

* * *

Graeme is usually one of the first players at the rink, but for our next game he is late. When we go out, he usually invites the rest of the guys along. The only time they come out is after a game, so they typically ask me for updates on the nights they miss. Of course, this time I have something to report. I tell them it was fun and that Graeme had hooked up with a young blond.

Without any help, they quickly figure out the details, and by the time Graeme gets to the rink everyone knows. In short order, he is talking about it without a hint of embarrassment.

Actually, Graeme had committed a crime in 49 states, but nobody is really judging him here, rather we all have a good laugh about it. Los Angeles is a very liberal place, so in a room full of guys nobody sees Graeme's actions as a moral issue. If I had still been living in the Bible belt, the conversation may have been much different, but I don't believe in protecting people from themselves. Naively, I think prostitution is a victimless crime.

CHAPTER 5 – QUE SARAH, SARAH

A couple of days after Graeme's pool party, I call Lindsay and ask for Sarah's phone number. She gives it to me and is very encouraging, so I call Sarah and set up a date. It takes two or three weeks to coordinate our schedules—not usually a good sign—but the reasons are legitimate. I am traveling back to North Carolina to see my kids, Kyndal and Johnathan, one weekend, and she was unavailable the next. We haven't seen each other in almost a month by the time we finally go out but still seem to be connecting. I'm feeling like a tourist in SoCal, and she wants to show me Long Beach, where she grew up.

A guided tour from an attractive woman sounds great except that she lives in her parents' guesthouse. Fortunately, the parents aren't home when I pick her up because I'm dreading the idea of answering any *age* questions. It's kind of silly because in another era, given our ages, I would have been dead and she considered an old maid. Sarah is 23, so dating her is both socially and legally acceptable. Nevertheless, I am thankful her parents aren't there, although I probably would have had a lot in common with them.

Our differences strike me as she shows me around, and I comment, "This is a really nice house."

"Thanks. We closed on it the day before the '94 riots broke out. We lost $100,000 equity overnight," she explains.

We? She was 11 years old when her parents bought the house, yet she considers it hers. I have already owned three houses of my own, and it has been a long time since I felt like I was part owner of my parents' house.

Still, I am attracted to this woman and she seems to be interested in me too. While I was in North Carolina, Lindsay had thrown a party to which George was invited. Sarah had spent much of the time plying him for information about me. Details of my life have filtered their way from Graeme to Lindsay to Sarah, but happily she doesn't seem to be aware of my mental breakdown. George and I figure out that even though I am a trustworthy Canadian, Graeme called his private investigator to pull some basic information about me. George was as vague as possible, but she had a lot of questions. *Is his real name Warren? Is he really 36? Was his divorce really bad? I can't believe he has two kids, does he really? Why did he move to Los Angeles?*

It is nice of George to give me warning that I am going to get grilled. George was also left with the impression that Sarah is looking for a serious boyfriend, so it is helpful not to get caught off guard by that.

We start with dinner at her favorite Japanese restaurant, which is loud and not at all intimate. It is perfect for avoiding questions, though. The food is good, and I have to remind myself to eat at my *date* pace, not my *one-pizza-in-a-room-full-of-guys pace.* Either I am successful, or she doesn't care about fast eating because after dinner she wants to show me more of her city. For dessert, we eat ice cream at the revitalized Long Beach shopping district and then go to the Queen Mary for drinks. It's a pleasant night, so we sit outside and get to know each other better.

I am determined to focus the conversation on her, thereby keeping it away from me. I get the details of how she met Lindsay, where she went to school, and what her job is. She also works at a day care, which means that she is into kids – not necessarily a good thing if you're just looking for casual relations.

Eventually she runs out of things to tell me, so I steer the conversation to our mutual friends. I am interested in the trip they had all taken together to Arizona. Graeme was playing in a big hockey tournament, and he paid Lindsay to go. Patrick and

Sarah decided that they also wanted to spend Memorial Day weekend in Phoenix. I had overheard Graeme inviting James at pickup one day, and I couldn't understand why he didn't go. The way Graeme presented it was that he was renting a van and filling it with five or six women. James, who had a girlfriend anyway, must have known that five or six in "Graeme-speak" really meant Lindsay and Sarah. James has since told me that Graeme always used hyperbole to build momentum for a group activity.

Sarah confides to me that she knows that Graeme is attracted to her, but she doesn't see him that way. At his pool party, I noticed him hitting on her but had written it off to his drunken stupor. She tells me that they shared a room together in Phoenix, but that they had separate beds. While Graeme was apparently the perfect gentleman, I imagine he probably had something more in mind. He had made a point of warning her about his snoring, to which she responded, "Yeah, don't worry about it, my grandpa snores a lot too."

Ouch. He was so mad that he wouldn't talk to her for the rest of the trip, and I can't say that I blame him. If she had started comparing me to her dad, our date would have been over. I don't tell her about Graeme's encounter with the hooker, but we agree that Graeme is desperate for female attention and is trying too hard.

I say, "From what I can tell, his ex-wife really did a number on his self-confidence. Did you ever meet her?"

"Oh yeah, she was a wild lady."

"What do you mean?"

"You know those morphine patches that they give you to wear after you've had major surgery?"

"Not really, but I get the idea."

"She used to wear two of those when she was just hanging around the house."

"Wow." No wonder Grant has drug problems. If Sarah can tell me something like that, then I feel comfortable asking what had happened to Graeme's ex. "How did she die?"

"Oh, you don't know." She seems very surprised, as if the circumstances of Julia's death are common knowledge.

"No." I hope that I don't sound overly eager.

"She overdosed."

"Jesus."

I sit there for a minute trying to process this information. I'm shocked, but then I'm irritated with myself for being shocked. Her house is filled with medications of every type. One of the pieces of furniture that is in my bedroom is a wobbly, piano-type bench with a storage compartment. Every time I sat on the bench, I heard a rattling noise. For a long time, I didn't think anything of it, but eventually I got curious. I opened the lid and found half-consumed bottles of Oxycontin and Methadone prescribed to Julia Bercham. This woman had so many drugs in her home that she had hidden them in benches and forgotten about them.

* * *

Living in a house with narcotics hidden all over is not the best situation for me. When Sandra underwent a laparoscopy for infertility in 1999, she was given a prescription for Percocet. They gave her more pills than she needed, but she didn't like the way the opiates altered her. I had heard that pharmaceuticals were becoming very popular with people wanting to get high without the stigma of using illicit drugs. The way pot or mushrooms made me feel wasn't worth the risk of getting arrested, so I was curious about these legal drugs.

I started experimenting, but it didn't go on for very long because we were focused on building our family. Occasionally, opiates were available due to a minor surgery or hockey injury, but I would never actively seek them out. My addiction was dormant for four years, but by 2003 the stress of school, job frustrations and a failing marriage were wearing on me. I started ordering enough Hydrocodone online to have the opiate high daily.

I knew enough about drug addiction to understand that the body builds up a tolerance, so more of the drug is required to get the same feeling. I would "cycle" on and off it, taking it for a few months then weaning myself off. I would let my body recover for a few months and then start using again. At the peak of my addiction, I took twelve pills in one day, but I have heard that big-time addicts will take as many as 100 per day.

I wonder what and how much Julia Bercham had to take to kill herself.

* * *

I get home to find Graeme sitting on the couch relaxing. It isn't the first time. His voice is weak, and his body language reminds me of my own when I was high on Hydrocodone. I ask him if he is loaded.

"No, I'm just really tired."

I can't be 100% certain that he is dipping into Julia's stash because he does work long hours, and his business is thriving. There is also a small possibility that he may have been crying, so I don't care to push him. Given that he is taking Viagra by the shovel, however, I question whether I should talk to him about getting some help. Of course that would be the height of hypocrisy, but I should do it anyway. Now I understand why my father was always able to tell exactly when I was on drugs. It's pretty obvious if you look at it objectively, and Graeme shows all the signs.

I think of how Grant and Ryan Bercham never really had a chance. Graeme told me that Ryan had always been *peculiar*, meaning he struggled with his identity, and perhaps that contributed to his destructive behaviors. Graeme often blamed the fall from his highchair for Grant's lack of impulse control because it had been serious enough to put him into a coma. The fact that both were raised in an environment of unrestrained financial privilege, which continued into adulthood, didn't help either. I suspect, however, that neither Grant's fall nor Ryan's sexuality had much to do with their problems. Rather, they simply inherited their parents' addictive personalities and continue the cycle of substance abuse. The Berchams are the most tragic family I have ever met.

On my date with Sarah, before she gave me the details of Julia's death, I had been carefully considering everything I said. The new information started my mind thinking about everything except our date. This, combined with a few cocktails, caused me to completely let my guard down. In the days leading up to the date, George and I had discussed at length strategies for how to handle the fact that Sarah was trying to snare a full-time boyfriend. I was absolutely not interested in that, but George was promoting that I should be nice to her so we could network through her circle of friends and meet lots of people. What he was really saying is that he didn't want me to taint his good name by pumping and dumping her.

Dating 101: do not mention to a girl that you promised your friend you'd be nice to her so you could find him dates – it doesn't make for pleasant conversation. I had made the comment in passing, but now with the clear light of day I realize why she cooled off so quickly. Maybe it had been on my part a subconscious zinger for the *Graeme grandpa* story, but I do feel bad for being so flippant. At least I got my questions about Julia's death answered without actually having to ask Graeme.

In hindsight, it is for the best that Sarah wants nothing to do with me, given her desire for a long-term relationship. In spite of my many issues, I've at least been able to avoid rebounding into another mistake. I might have gone out with her for a while and then slowly distanced myself when it got too serious, which is how I ended my first post-divorce relationship. I met a single mom who took all of a week to tell me that she thought I was the perfect man. I was in the worst phase of my drug abuse, but if I had asked her to marry me, she would have.

Women generally see me as a potential provider rather than a fling, which is regrettable seeing I feel that I am, right now, screwed up and clearly attracting the wrong people. This new picture I have of Graeme's family life disturbs me, and I begin to think that my new friend falls into the category of wrong people. Nevertheless, I love living in his house, and I am tapped into his social network. I also don't believe that his problems can affect me.

CHAPTER 6 – ANGER ISSUES

By late July, I had been working at Disney for about three weeks, but the situation was deteriorating. I had worked as a computer programmer for ten years and was amazed how difficult it was to get the data that I needed. That combined the normal job stress, and the Valium I had stolen from Graeme resulted in my abrupt departure from the company.

Life sometimes rewards bad behavior. My rash, drug-influenced decision to quit the Disney job has turned out to be a blessing. Granted, I am unemployed again and can't put the Disney job on my resume, but in early August, I was able to take a nine day Canadian vacation with my kids, rather than just our typical weekend visit. It really sunk in just how much I missed them, and I enjoyed every moment of that trip. It was more valuable to me than any job could ever be, and I would do the same thing again. Being their father again was a powerful experience that if I had been further along in my recovery, I may have been convinced to move back to North Carolina. I am still so bitter about the way things have turned out for me, however, that I don't consider this an option. I don't want to be anywhere near Raleigh or the other people I associated with it. Nevertheless, my time in Canada was a turning point for me.

Now that I'm back in L.A., I've begun anew to try to resurrect my career. Graeme winced when I told him about my decision to leave Disney. Given our friendship, he was probably concerned that I had taken a step backwards; however, he also has selfish reasons for wanting me to get reestablished financially. Until Julia died, Graeme kept his residence and law office in a three-bedroom townhouse about three miles south of Hollywood. After her death, the business stayed there, but only until he could do some fix-ups and rent it. We have an understanding that part of my free rent deal is that I pay rent in the townhouse after three months.

Graeme's townhouse is very nice, and I like the idea of living there in spite of the somewhat dicey location. I also feel that it is a fair arrangement because I have put in fewer hours working on his house than what we had originally agreed. If I can find a roommate, the terms will be better than anything else available. The problem is that I can't justify the whole cost by myself, and the only person I know in L.A. who is looking for a new place is George. Graeme has suggested several times that I try to persuade him, but when I spoke to George, he immediately dismissed the idea. He wants to live somewhere *cool* and has his mind set on Beverly Hills. I've had to tell Graeme that George will not be a part of the rental arrangement, so Graeme is pissed off at George, and what had been a casual friendship has become adversarial.

We can table the issue for now because I'm not moving until October, and Graeme has a more pressing concern. He and I have not only hockey and bad marriages in common but also business failures, although his is on a much larger scale. Graeme applied his degrees in engineering and law to work as real estate consultant. Because of the explosive growth, rugged terrain, and earthquake risks in Southern California his business was once very lucrative. He built a large consulting practice, which did well enough for a number of years to justify rapid expansion. In order to finance the payroll growth, he had leveraged, but when the Los Angeles metro area was struck by 1994's Northridge earthquake, the local economy was devastated. With the rest of the country expanding Californians left in droves, and the real estate market suffered. Graeme's business could no longer support the payroll, and he declared bankruptcy.

Graeme declared bankruptcy, but Julia's property was unaffected. He was shrewd enough to have used their legal separation to protect the assets they had accumulated during the boom. Basically, all the assets except his residence and car were in her name, and creditors couldn't touch anything. Her death now presents problems that go beyond the apparent emotional impact. Everything was willed to Ryan, but the creditors sued Graeme because they calculated that they could prove he was actually in control of them. Graeme thinks that there is a real danger of losing this case, and it is for this reason that we are now cataloguing his artwork.

This past weekend, Graeme traveled to Napa Valley to work with Sotheby's to sell select pieces from his art collection. He boasts of his eye for art, and in fact many of his purchases have turned out to be wise investments. He has more than enough to cover the potential $200,000 judgment against him. While he was in Napa, he was also romantically pursuing the 24-year-old art broker, Mary, who is helping him put his collection on the market. I can tell from the way he describes the situation that she is only interested in him professionally; however, she did let him take her out and pay for everything.

Meanwhile, I'm, once again, beginning to get some interest in my resume. The most serious of the inquiries came from the biotech firm Amgen for two different positions, both of which would be located northwest of L.A. in Thousand Oaks. On paper, the company is fabulous, but I'm not sure I want to live that far away from the friends I'm beginning to make. The location, however, became irrelevant when I realized, during an interview, that Amgen has some of the most obnoxious employees one could hope to meet. One of the fellows asked me, in front of a panel of his peers, what I would do if I were in the top floor of a building and there was a terrorist attack. I felt like grabbing him by the throat and throttling him for asking such an inflammatory, ridiculous question. What if I or someone else in the room had lost a family member on 9/11? Instead, I reigned myself in, gave a carefully measured response, but the correct one would have been, "I would jump out the window and use you to break my fall."

Obviously, that position wasn't a fit, and I've told the recruiter that I am no longer interested in applying to Amgen. The trip out to Thousand Oaks wasn't a complete waste of time, though. I proved that I could control my emotions in the face of blatant provocation, and I also got a much-needed cover story.

Back from Napa, Graeme's attention is focused on trying to get the townhouse situation resolved. In Graeme's mind, Grant is the solution to the roommate problem. Grant has gone through many relationships, and my understanding is that they almost always end in some sort of domestic violence. I am sure that the prison time Grant served was due to a domestic assault charge. Moreover, every time I talk to him his relationship with his current girlfriend/ex/fiancée has changed. They are engaged one week and then broken up the next. Then they are back together, and there are rumors of a pregnancy. I know that she would become part of the package, and I have no interest in dealing with that drama. Plus, having cleaned up after Grant once, I know that I can't handle doing it for an extended period.

Graeme keeps pushing the Grant-as-roommate issue , so I end up telling him that I got a contract position at Amgen and will be moving out in that direction. I don't like lying to someone who has been so generous to me, but there is no fucking way that I'm going to live with Grant. I'm not that desperate for danger. Ironically, with me out as a possible roommate, Grant and his girlfriend/ex/fiancée have rented an apartment together, which is two blocks from Amgen. What are the chances? This is extremely awkward; I'll need to keep my wits about me and deflect all questions about my job.

CHAPTER 7 – PLAYOFFS

Graeme was disappointed that I wasn't going to rent his place, but he has been very gracious about it. He has continued to let me stay with him through the end of September even though he's asking very little of me around the house. Besides, hockey is still the most important thing in his life, and that is going extremely well. The Culver summer hockey season is winding down, and our team is in the running for the championship. Culver has a pretty straightforward naming system: White (us), Black, Green, Orange, Yellow, and Red. We are third in the six-team league, with the top four teams making the playoffs. Moreover, we have beaten every team at least once, so our chances are as good as anybody's. Graeme has spent several years building this team and has never won a championship. He doesn't want to do anything to screw it up.

To the best of my knowledge Graeme has never won a hockey championship of any kind, and I think that this is due in large part to his coaching philosophy. The most effective hockey teams are well-balanced, top to bottom. The ability to send out one line after another and wear the other team down is what wins games. Occasionally, a tremendous individual effort can be enough to win a game when your team is outplayed, but this is the exception. Every team will have a top line, but good teams have a second line that is basically just as good. On championship teams, every line makes a meaningful contribution.

Graeme learned somewhere that teams should load up their top line, so he always puts all his top players on one line. He loves having a star line, and he pampers them to the extent that he creates a trio of prima donnas, which is difficult to do in a recreational league. For him the second line is an afterthought – even though he is playing on it – and his teams typically finish last. I joined his team midway through the season and am happy to play on any line, including the second one. This balances out the lines to the extent that the second line is probably better than the first.

Right now the team is on a roll, with the playoffs in sight, and apparently Graeme is rolling too. I went to Edmonton for a childhood friend's wedding, and when I got back Graeme told me about his latest trip to the B.W. Apparently, he was sitting at the bar when an Australian girl struck up a conversation.

"I know you. You're Graeme."

Graeme didn't even need to finish the rest of the story because I immediately knew what happened—he'd been marked. The first hooker had described him to her colleagues, and this one, named Kendra, had recognized him. With Graeme's fragile self-esteem, he viewed the attention as positive. In his mind, it simply gave him a whole new group of *friends* to talk to, so this casual conversation turned into an ongoing relationship.

He was beside himself as he talked about it. "She gave me a freebie," he boasted.

"Yeah right," I knew there had to be a catch. "Nothing is ever free, especially with hookers."

"No, we really hit it off, and she told me she was having a slow night."

"There's more to the story," I said. There had to be because Graeme isn't exactly the Richard Gere type.

"No, trust me. Life is good baby." He was emphatic, but I didn't believe it for a second.

He has continued to see her for the past few weeks, and gradually I've gotten the rest of the story. Discretion not being his strong suit, Graeme must have told the first hooker, Kendra's friend, that he is an attorney. Kendra had gotten herself into some trouble with a DUI, and they worked out a deal in which Graeme will represent her in that case. I have to admit that it seems like a pretty good deal for him, but I've started to lock my things up. Most of my valuables are in storage, but Kendra is coming over all the time, and occasionally, she brings a friend. Sooner or later something bad is going to happen.

I am usually in bed by the time she comes over, so it is a few weeks before I finally meet her. She seems nice enough, but I don't find her at all attractive. I try to be cordial, but she likely feels that I'm judging her because I quickly excuse myself and go to my room. It's nothing personal, but I really have no desire to socialize with her and Graeme – it's just too weird for me. After I fall asleep, I'm disturbed by a commotion in the kitchen but can't tell what's going on.

The next day, I ask Graeme what all the noise was about. He explains that Kendra had gotten upset and freaked out; she apparently wants out of the business. He eventually calmed her down, and she was fine by the time she left. I honestly hope that I didn't cause her meltdown with my avoidance behavior, because I realize that hookers are people too, most of them anyway.

I feel the need to say something to get him to back off a little bit.

"What's the attraction?"

"She's fun. We're having fun." Nice way of putting it.

Unlike Graeme, I think about the repercussions if he gets caught in his little arrangement; he's really setting himself up to be extorted. I mention that he could be disbarred for doing this pro-boner work, but he just laughs it off. Like so many before him, his arrogance is his Achilles heel. He believes that he is too smart and in control to suffer the consequences of risky behavior.

* * *

When the regular season ends, we are in third place as expected. Yellow is comfortably in first, and Green and Red are out. Our first round game is against Black, who have finished just two points ahead of us in the standings. Black against White. Every team has another team that they just don't match up against well, and for us it is Black. It has nothing to do with talent because we probably have more – they play as a team.

As a follow-up to the selling of his artwork collection, Graeme actually has to miss the game for another trip to Napa. I know that he has to be in serious need of getting the money out of his art, or he would never have missed such an important game against our nemesis. He talks about winning that championship every day. Graeme is our weakest player, so not having him at the game should actually be helpful. Unfortunately, without him there is no clear leader. He asked me to be in charge, but I am new to the team and therefore not accepted as captain in

Graeme's absence. To make matters worse, we have eleven skaters show up for the game.

Having an extra player can be a nice advantage because you can get your forwards extra rest in a quick paced game. If you have a selfish group of players, however, eleven is the absolute worst number. First, you have to decide who the extra player is, and then he has to rotate through the lines, each player taking a turn missing a shift. I also decide to mix the lines up a little bit because I want to make sure that we have at least two strong skaters on each line. This juggling meets with resistance from one player in particular, Andy, who clearly feels it is beneath him to play with many of the team members.

In spite of all the drama, we actually jump out to the lead, and outplay our Black rival. By the end of the first period, however, the lines have to be rearranged to accommodate egos. The second period is a draw, and we are up 4-2 going into the third period. Unfortunately, most of the forwards are refusing to take their turns sitting, and I have to spend more energy on managing the lines than playing the game. My anger management is better but still not good enough to tolerate infantile behavior from a group of grown men who are worrying more about counting ice-time than trying to win the game. They can't or won't realize that if we win the game, everybody gets more ice time.

I decide that to relieve my headache, and avoid wrapping my stick around somebody's head, I'll sit the rest of the game. I have played in enough elite hockey games that I'm not going to live and die by a recreational league result, so I leave. It must have been the correct decision because White holds on and defeats Black 4-3. Meanwhile, in the other semi-final fourth-place Orange upset Gold, so at long last the stars are aligned for Graeme to get his shot at the title.

When he gets back from Napa, I inform him that I won't be playing in the final, but his two great strengths are persuasion and mediation. He begs me to play the final game and promises that he will take care of all egos, mine included I suppose. He is not the type of guy to resort to threats, and I have to respect him for that. He could have told me to play or pack my bags, but it just isn't in his make-up to do that. He promises me that some players won't be back for the winter season, and that is enough. I owe it to him, so I agree to finish the job. My playing on his hockey team means more to Graeme than anything I could do around his house and is—I'm clear on this now— the real reason he has invited me into his home.

The next week, we pound Orange and became the Culver City Hockey League "A" division champions. After the game, I shake hands with the other team and immediately leave the ice. I find a dressing room, quickly change, and exit the rink before the rest of the team has even finished their on-ice celebrations. I am so disgusted with some of the players on that team that I want nothing to do with the trophy presentations or team pictures. Rationally, I understand what my behavior means; I am still overreacting to things, and this is just another example of that. I've been this way my entire life, so why change now? The drugs aren't helping my mood control either.

The rest of the team goes out to the bar to celebrate, so I'm not surprised when Graeme comes waltzing in around 2 a.m. Still not working, I am on a night-owl schedule, and I have my door open when he gets home.

"You should have stayed for the picture," he says with clear disappointment in his voice.

"Graeme, it was all I could do not to beat the fuck out of Andy as it was. The only reason I played was because I felt that I owed it to you." Part of me had wanted to celebrate with Graeme, but I am still seething over the ridiculousness in the semi-final game.

"I know, and I appreciate that. I brought you your hat," he says enthusiastically, as though I should have been thrilled.

"I don't want that; it's a piece of crap."

"Take it. It's nice." I take the hat, but there is nothing nice about it. It looks like something a farmer would have worn in the mid-70s. Graeme is absolutely beaming as he wears his, so I accept his gesture. I don't want to dampen his spirits, but even if I had wanted to I couldn't have managed to bring him down: first *free* sex and now the treasured championship hat.

CHAPTER 8 – CRACK HO

The break between the summer and winter season is three weeks, which includes Labor Day. Out of the blue, my parents decide to trade up from their Canmore, Alberta condominium to a vacation home on the river. My mother is in poor health, and given that I am free these days, they fly me up to help them move. It is nice to be able to help them out with the big job after all they have done for me, and coincidentally that trip also marks the beginning of the end of my prescription drug abuse.

When I get back, Graeme has more good news in his life. He has reached a settlement with his creditors for an amount that is very satisfactory to him. It must have happened quickly because a week earlier he had asked me if anyone had ever questioned me while I was out front of the house. I told him I'd never been approached in such a way, but he wanted me to plan for the possibility if I ever were. He asked me not to tell anyone anything because I might inadvertently give creditors ammunition for the case. I assured him that I could handle that, but still he was concerned, almost paranoid.

Now the case is officially over, and he wants to celebrate. He is even more excited to tell me about the new woman he met. It's beginning to seem as though his most interesting evenings happen while I'm out of town. He had gone out to the B.W. with Lindsay, and she had gotten extremely drunk. As they were leaving, this new mystery woman started chatting him up. Graeme was intrigued, so he quickly poured Lindsay into a cab and went back inside. Apparently, there had been an instant connection, and he and this new woman are now an item.

"Wait until you see her. She's 25 and an absolute knockout. And get this, she's black." He adds the part about her race as though I'm supposed to be impressed. I find it curious that he is somehow awed by her skin color because he has often referred to his backyard neighbors as *niglets*, which implies more disrespect than awe. Now, he's excited because this chick is black. I assume that this provides him with a huge ego boost because it somehow makes him feel like a player.

Always the cynic, I have to ask, "Is she another hooker?"

"No. Her father is one of Seattle's biggest selling real-estate brokers. She's down here trying to get into the business." He is adamant that she isn't a whore.

"Did she see you pick up the tab?" Maybe she isn't a hooker, but I am guessing that she's after him for his money.

"Yeah, why?"

"No offense, but you're usually not the type of guy who is picked up by young, black chicks. She obviously noticed that you have money."

"You're probably right, but I don't care. The sex is unbelievable; she's like a sexual predator. I've never experienced anything like this." A very telling choice of words.

I assume he meant to use a word like tigress rather than predator. He definitely picked up on something subconscious. Given that they already had sex and she hadn't charged him, he had good reason to believe that she wasn't a professional. For me, however, it's not adding up. Why would a young, supposedly attractive, rich woman pick Graeme up in a bar? I hint at this in a diplomatic way, but I haven't even met her so my suspicions mean very little to him.

There is a Los Angeles radio host, Tom Leykis, who made his controversial claim to fame by teaching men how to date. Many women revile him because he has no tolerance for those who use men for money. He has been labeled a misogynist because his advice includes things like:

- Do not get married. There is absolutely no advantage for a man to get married; it only contractually relieves him of half of his assets.
- Do not ever spend more than $40 on a date. You can ensure this by eating a hearty meal before you go out and then ordering a salad. No woman will ever eat more than her date.
- Talk as little as possible because anything you say can and will be used against you. You might talk your way out of getting laid (see Sarah).
- As soon as they start whining, cajoling, or manipulating, dump them immediately. Moreover, if they haven't slept with you by the third date, dump them because they have no plan to ever sleep with you.

I have listened to Leykis a few times primarily for the humorous battles that he has with angry women who call his show. His rules are not rocket science, and most guys instinctively know the general idea of what he's saying; not Graeme though. I know that he is aware of the Leykis rules, but he still likes to spend a lot of money on women in the desperate hope that they will date him. Now that he has a woman he is completely infatuated with, there is no telling how much money he will spend on her. I bring up the Leykis rules almost daily because it is a glib way of reminding him not to get relieved of his cash.

Very quickly, Graeme cut Kendra off and is now dating Jasmine exclusively; however, she is not dating him exclusively. She has at least one other relationship Graeme is aware of, and it is with a well-known actor of *The Breakfast Club* fame. He even manages to turn this piece of information into an ego-pump. He, Graeme, is digging the same ditch as a world-famous actor. It is clear from the way he describes the situation that she has no intention of cutting the actor off, but as long as Graeme is getting his, he is happy. That's what he keeps telling himself and anyone who'll listen, anyway.

For two weeks now, I haven't met the mysterious Jasmine because she avoids me. I'll pull up to the house, see them in the kitchen, and by the time I get inside they are gone to Graeme's room. When I point out that she obviously isn't very friendly, Graeme is happy to explain her behavior.

"It's because she's always naked. She just loves to walk around naked. Even if we're just hanging out in the living room doing a crossword puzzle, she doesn't like wearing clothes."

Goddamn he was blind, "She's manipulating you."

"No she's just very free with her body," he says this more for himself than for me. It is irritating that he refuses to acknowledge to himself that she is only walking around the house naked to control him.

This behavior of Graeme's is another notable example of something I first became aware of in high school: people believe what they want to believe, regardless of the truth. This is particularly true when it concerns men ignoring things about women to whom they are attracted. I had a conflict with a friend's girl, and he got caught in the middle. It wasn't an easy thing to tell a buddy that his girlfriend was a liar, but I felt that I needed to.

When I gave him the details of our conflict he said, "That's not what she told me, and she's my girlfriend so I have to believe her." To me it was not *have to* but rather *choose to*. We are friends to this day because, on some level, he knew that she was lying. I learned from that high school experience, and many others since, so I can usually tell when someone is ignoring facts for emotional reasons. Because Graeme is making a semi-conscious choice to ignore the obvious, nothing I say will make a difference.

Finally, one evening in mid-September, I have the distinct pleasure of meeting the elusive, naked cowgirl. She doesn't want to meet me but she gets caught in the kitchen, fully clothed, when I happen to be there. Graeme can't wait to show her off, so he quickly introduces us. She gives me a fake smile, a pathetic fingertip handshake, and pretends to be friendly as briefly as she can. If she had tolerated me for about two seconds, slowly curled her lip, and then tried to bite my hand I would have had more respect for her. At least Pumpkin was honest when she nipped at me. I know immediately that the only reason she tolerates my presence is because she doesn't dare reveal her true nature to Graeme.

I don't care. I only have a couple of weeks left in the house, and I'm not going to let this fucking bitch ruin a friendship. Besides, I have just gotten some great news of my own. A couple of nights earlier, I was up late when an email came through from a recruiter. She wanted me to interview for a contract-to-hire position the next morning. It is highly unusual, but in five days, I start a new job at NBCUniversal.

From 1983 until 2005 my favorite TV shows were first *Cheers*, then *Seinfeld*, and finally *Friends*. Before I accepted the job at Disney, I had some interest from NBCU, but I didn't pursue it because Disney moved hastily to give me an offer. I knew I couldn't afford to screw around and squander a solid offer from Disney for the mere chance of a position at NBCU. Now, completely unexpected, I am going to be working for the company that has provided me with so much entertainment. As Graeme would say, "Life is good, baby!"

On the same day I accept the NBCU job, our new hockey season starts. California is full of talented athletes, and when Gretzky came to town, many of them began playing hockey. They weren't well taught, however, and most of the California players now playing in the men's leagues around L.A. essentially play roller hockey on ice. Individual one-on-one play, dipsy-doodle moves, and posing are the hallmarks of this style. Puck movement is viewed as a last resort. Technically, Andy is a Canadian but he plays hockey Cali-style. For the new season, Graeme kicks him off the team and replaces him with two new Canadians, Jay and James. They play with Canadian heart and are willing to play with anybody, so we now have three solid lines. Easily the best team in the league, we win our first three games handily. By the end of our third game, Graeme is getting full credit for the team that he had built.

"People are starting to notice us," he said as we skated off the ice after a win.

"Well I would hope so, we're the defending champions, and we've won seven games in a row," I was a little irritated because I realized that the guys on the other teams thought our championship a fluke.

"Well now they're really talking about us," he emphasized. There is nothing that Graeme likes better than to be talked about; in fact, it is what is most important to him.

So, life is good baby, and we both seem to be getting what we want. In Graeme's situation, however, I can't help but think that it is a case of be careful what you ask for. Within a couple of weeks, he has become completely consumed by this woman. I realize that it isn't just about the sex because he had been with Kendra for at least a month. Instead, it is all about the status. Jasmine is much better looking than Kendra, and when he is with her he gets noticed. Even when he isn't with her, he uses her to get noticed. She let him take a nude picture of her, from the neck down, with his camera phone. Wherever we go, Graeme makes a point of steering the conversation to his girlfriend and gracing everybody with a look at her picture. He seems to have no shame, so I feel the embarrassment for him.

Another lesson I learned in high school was that when guys start to get into women, they stop caring about sports. A lot of talented players I knew stopped playing after high school because they had serious girlfriends. According to Sarah, Graeme had actually given up the game for a time and had only started playing again about two years ago. She said that he looked much better and had lost a lot of weight since he started playing again. He never mentions that he took a break from hockey, but regardless, it is now his primary source of recreation. I know that if he starts skipping hockey, Jasmine is taking over his life.

I feel like I am giving him a useful frame of reference when I say, "You'll know when you've crossed the line with this chick. When you start missing hockey for her then you've gone off the deep end. And when that happens, I want you to think back to this conversation."

He just laughs, and I know that the advice has been ignored as quickly as it's given.

CHAPTER 9 – RULE NUMBER ONE

I am thrilled to be working for NBCU, and I haven't been this excited about my career since the early planning stages of Second Wind. When I was brand new to the corporate world, I felt like I had made it. Information Technology was red-hot because the Internet was quickly changing the world. The career path was bourgeoning, so pay increases and promotions came often. There was also the ever-present dream of becoming a stock-option millionaire, and as a group, we got spoiled. Then, the bubble burst, and employers seemed to take pleasure in their newfound power. If you didn't like their employment terms, there were ten programmers from India waiting to take your place. I didn't like their employment terms, so I let the ten Indians take my place and struck out on my own. Four years later, I accepted that being a corporate drone wasn't so bad if it came with a steady paycheck.

By the time I was ready to return to the corporate world, my interest in IT had long since faded, so I needed a new career. I chose to switch to finance because I had grown up around it. Most people, I believe, eventually become one or both of their parents. As much as we might rebel, we can't deny who we are. Once Ryan Bercham developed a sense of purpose in his life, he decided to pursue a degree in philosophy because he knew that it would be good preparation for law school. As I was following my father's footsteps into finance, Ryan was trying to follow his father's into law. Grant, unfortunately, was following his mother's path.

My first few weeks at NBCU are intense because I received very little training from, ironically, the Indian that I am replacing. I am working in the Universal Studios Hollywood (USH) division, and there are supposed to be two Financial Analysts in my group. Unfortunately, I am by myself and it seems that the situation will remain that way for the foreseeable future. So, I very much need my sleep on the weekends, and am cranky if I don't get it. The weekend before I'm scheduled to move out, I'm trying to sleep in. I can't though, because every 30 seconds I hear the fingernails-on-the-chalkboard sound of Pumpkin squawking to get into to Graeme's room. The problem is that it no longer belongs to Graeme. It now belongs to Jasmine, and the African princess isn't about to tolerate animals where she sleeps. Poor Pumpkin has been out-diva'd and is relegated to the entryway in front of Graeme's door.

I hate divas, so I don't feel a bit sorry for her. After an hour of yipping, I have had enough and get out of bed with every intention of turning her into a slipper – the dog not Jasmine. Luckily for her, she is quick enough to avoid all but a few glancing smacks. In March, when Graeme's house will become a crime-scene, she will use that same agility to keep animal control officers at bay for 20 minutes.

My father used to joke around with me and say, "Never get married."

He would usually make this statement when my mother was bitching at him, so I found it humorous. When Grant almost ran us over in the driveway, Graeme educated me on his theory on children. He spoke emphatically and slowly, like I should be hanging on every word, "Rule number one: never have kids. Rule number two: if you break rule number one, lock them in a box and don't let them out."

I don't find Graeme's rules humorous at all because I love my kids to the point of pain. Perhaps the fact that conceiving with Sandra had been difficult makes me more appreciative of them. We tried for two years and finally had to resort to In Vitro fertilization, which did not go smoothly. Sandra didn't produce many eggs, and of the ones she did only four that fertilized were deemed viable for implant. On the day of the transfer, I got to view the eight-cell embryos under the microscope. We were told quite clearly that the chances of all of them surviving were very low, but if they did, we would have had to do selective reduction. This is a euphemistic way of saying that you have to terminate two of your children.

Sandra was adamant that she would not abort, and it would have been a truly horrible decision to make: play God and lower the risk for two children or take a chance on all four. Nature took care of the decision for us and I am grateful for that, but I will always wonder about those other two embryos. Could we have managed four? Would they look like their siblings? Would they be boys or girls? I have no way of even knowing which of the cell collections that I viewed survived and became our beautiful twins.

Sandra's entire pregnancy was unpleasant: she had nausea for most of it, there was no *horny* phase, and we spent the most of it focused on reaching the important milestones of what was a high-risk pregnancy. When we reached week 24, we were relieved because babies can survive if born premature. By 31 weeks, the survival rate is high, and by 34 weeks the probability of having healthy babies is high. With twins, because they mature faster in the womb, birth after 36 weeks is considered normal, and the babies can be taken home without spending time in intensive care.

When we first found out we were having twins, Sandra told me that she wanted to enjoy every moment of the journey, even if she was feeling poorly. I was to remind her of this every time she complained about any aspect of the pregnancy. By the third trimester, reality set in, and she told me to shut up if I followed her initial instructions. We had made it to 35 weeks and four days when things started to happen. Shortly before we were to have to get up to go to work, she was feeling particularly crappy and yelled something at me from the bathroom. It sounded a lot like more whining, so it didn't register.

"My water broke!" She yelled, and thus began the most vivid day of my life.

I proceeded to have a sitcom moment as I jumped up out of bed then zigged and zagged my way around the bedroom trying to decide what to do. Eventually, I decided to peek into the bathroom to see what was happening. Another sitcom moment ensued when we decided that I needed to bring her the phone so she could ask her sister what to do. Sandra was under the impression that the water would somehow shut off but was quickly told to get off the toilet and go to the hospital, as it would not.

I will never forget that early morning drive to Swedish Medical Center in Englewood, CO. I have never been as focused on my driving as I was that day, and I got us safely to the hospital. The children were delivered by C-section and then spent a few brief hours in neo-natal intensive care. By the evening, they were deemed to be healthy enough to come into our room.

I spent a good part of the day ferrying them around from examination to examination, but I was never really able to absorb the significance of what had happened. Then, that evening after Sandra's parents arrived in our room, I got a chance to sit with and truly experience my son. I was standing up holding him with his face on my chest when he decided to try and figure out this giant being that was holding him. With great effort he tilted his head back to look up at my face, and our eyes locked. I saw my own eyes looking back at me, and from that moment on we were connected.

It took longer to feel the same way about Kyndal because she had a rougher start to her life. It was tough for me to watch her scream in agony from her milk allergy. I was never able to soothe her, and for a month we didn't really bond. Eventually it happened though, and I love the different ways that I relate to them. I watch Johnathan play hockey, and when he gets close enough to where I'm sitting I can see him beaming through the cage of his facemask. Winning or losing he's got a smile on his face. The joy of chasing the puck is enough to wipe all his challenges away. Kyndal, on the other hand, hates sports. I once cobbled together a set of hockey equipment for her so that she could come out and play with Johnathan and me. All she could focus on was that the gloves were slimy. Such a problem had never even occurred to me, but she dealt with it anyway so that we could do something together. That she tolerates sports odors for me is a true display of love.

Perhaps, Graeme initially felt as strongly about his children as I do of mine, and perhaps if I had Grant Bercham for a son, I might feel differently about Graeme's rules. Grant can't or won't stop buying dogs, but of course, he doesn't take care of them once he gets them. Graeme doesn't have the heart to see them at the pound, so when Grant is done with them, he comes to the rescue. After five iterations of this game, Graeme has let Grant turn him into the male equivalent of the Crazy Cat Lady. His home is always kept up by his cleaning lady, but the faint scent of seven dogs marking their territory is always present.

Of all the dogs under Graeme's roof, Pumpkin is the only one that originally belonged to him. With such lofty status, expulsion from the bedroom is too much for her to abide. My threat to her life only keeps her quiet for fifteen minutes, so I give up. I decide to get up and go to the gym. When I get back, Jasmine is gone and Graeme is in the kitchen reading the newspaper. He definitely looks to me like a guy who is on top of the world. With my three months at Graeme's coming to an end, I've found a Hollywood Hills apartment close to work that allows Sherwood. Graeme seems like he is going to miss having me around because he tells me that I can stay as long as I want. Maybe he knows that there is no way I will accept, and he is trying to seem magnanimous. I choose to believe that the offer is genuine. We banter for a few more minutes, but he seems distracted by something else.

Finally, he tells me, "I kind of broke the Leykis rules."

"How?"

"I lent Jasmine $9000."

Kind of broke? Try shattered. "You know that you're never going to see that money again, don't you?"

"No, we have an agreement," he protested. How could a well-educated man be so stupid?

"Graeme. That money is gone. You'll never see it again." I really don't care if I piss him off. He needs to hear this.

"You're probably right, but I've done a cost-benefit analysis, and it's worth it. I have never had sex like this in my life." So Graeme is essentially paying her for sex now.

"Why does she need $9000?" I ask.

"She's got bad credit, and she needs to get set up with an apartment. I lent her the money and co-signed for her apartment."

Bad credit, what a fucking shock. "What about her father? I thought he was loaded."

"He cut her and her mother off," he said defensively.

A million questions are going through my mind. Why did he cut her off? Why didn't it worry Graeme that her behavior has been so horrendous that she gets cut off by her father? While it's obvious that his bitch has no use for me, I have even less for her. Even before I met her, the situation had sirens blaring in my head, which intensified the instant I met her. I implore him not to get hung up on her and to bail out after he has had some fun. I also tell him that he should not memorize her phone number, but rather keep it only in his contact list. Then when he is done with her, he can just delete the number and never have the temptation of calling her again.

Already, she has her hooks deep enough into him that he simply says, "You know I won't do that."

The sirens turn into five-alarm bells when he tells me about her life goals. She has made it clear to Graeme that she plans on having children within the next three years. It's obvious to me that she's trying to trap him into financing her and a kid for the next eighteen years. He doesn't believe this is an issue because all of the assets are in Ryan's name and there would be nothing for her to touch. I counter that, at the very least, he'd be liable for child support payments. He discounts that too because he is wearing rubbers, and she has assured him that she isn't looking to get pregnant right away. She goes as far as to make a big production of taking her birth control pills right in front of him. He acknowledges that these performances are completely transparent, but he still doesn't care.

He actually appears to enjoy it when I call him an idiot. He even starts prefacing his stories that way, "Yeah, I know I'm an idiot, but..."

You can't help those who don't want to be helped.

In time, I put the pieces together. She is most likely the illegitimate child of a horny rich guy, and being *cut-off* means that he has stopped paying child support. I don't know if Graeme will ever figure this out, but I doubt he would care even if he does. It is only a matter of time before Jasmine finds a horny, rich guy to knock her up, but as long as Graeme keeps getting great sex, nothing else matters. I wonder how much money Jasmine's mother has gotten out of her father.

If Graeme does manage to become a father again, it's going to put a lot of pressure on his relationship with his adult children. After only three short weeks of Graeme dating Jasmine, a conflict with Ryan is already gaining steam. During another of our kitchen conversations, Graeme relates the details of an argument.

"Ryan said to me, 'Dad, she's black!' I told him that that is a great way to lose a father." He is pointing at me for emphasis, which I suspect he had been doing during the original conversation.

Ryan was stating the obvious and perhaps showing a racist bone, but I think he was saying something a little deeper. I feel like he has encapsulated everything I have been telling Graeme in three simple words, and I find Graeme's response to his son very troubling.

"I don't know Graeme, I would never let a woman come between my children and me. You need to get your priorities straight."

"But she makes me happy, and my sons need to accept her," Graeme justifies.

At face value, he is correct, and I'm sure his sons would be thrilled if he did find someone who made him happy. Ryan probably senses what I do, however, that making Graeme happy is extremely low on Jasmine's priority list. Getting what she wants, regardless of the consequences, is what's at the top.

CHAPTER 10 – AVALANCHE

When I was about ten years old, I was looking through my grandparents' old photos and came across one that intrigued me. It was my Gramps with some of his siblings, and there was a slender young boy who had been about eight years old in the picture.

"Who's this?" I asked Gramps.

He studied the picture for a moment and then said, "That's Uncle Bud."

Wait a minute, I thought. Something's not right here, "but when did he get fat?"

Gramps let out an amused chuckle that he quickly stifled, but I could see in his eyes that he was still amused. "Well," he paused for a couple of beats to consider, "I guess when he started drinking beer."

Twenty years before the low-carb craze, my grandfather already knew that beer made you fat. There is still little scientific evidence to show that beer drinkers are more prone to abdominal obesity, but we all know better. People have always known what can happen if we let our vices get out of control.

By the summer of 2003, our Curves franchise was doing well, and I was free to spend most of my time on the MBA program. Even though the job market was extremely tough, I probably could have found another corporate IT job if I had wanted to, but I didn't. I was halfway through the MBA program and was already looking for finance related positions. Unfortunately, I hadn't progressed far enough to compete for that type of job. The program was geared for people working full-time, so I had plenty of spare time. I was bored, I felt trapped, and I wanted to escape.

When I first started chasing my tail, I would wait until late in the evening and reward myself for a productive day. I'd take the pill and wait. As the drug started to kick-in, I'd feel a rush of euphoria. Then, the drug would penetrate every cell in my body and take me to a dark place that I loved. My addiction progressed undetected because I had the time to do whatever I wanted. If I had had a full-time job, I wouldn't have been able to keep it up while taking ten Vicodins a day.

I've always tried to make sure that my self-esteem depended on much more than my career, but being unemployed was still difficult. Working for USH had a very positive impact on my psyche, and I felt much better about myself. I worked my ass off to get my contract position converted to permanent. I knew that I would not succeed if I were using drugs every day. The final step in pulling back from the abyss was moving out of Graeme's house and into my own apartment where there are no drugs unless I put them there.

There was no particular epiphany where I said, "I'm free of drugs!" Rather, I've been motivated to succeed again, and I know that the drugs would get in the way. These three months that I've been on contract have been the hardest that I've ever worked in a corporate position. I couldn't do that if I was using, and succeeding at the job is more important to me. It is that simple. I want to do well, and I'll do whatever it takes to accomplish that.

For the first couple of weeks after I move out, I have very little to do with Graeme. I have grown tired of his relationship with Jasmine and really don't want to hear any more about how gorgeous she is. To me, she's just another moderately attractive gold digger. Maybe, I should cut off all contact with Graeme, but I do miss hanging out and talking hockey with him. I am also concerned about him, and there are a lot reasons that I can't just abandon him. First, I have a sense of loyalty to the man who helped me get back on my feet. Second, we were on the same hockey team and unless I quit the team I will theoretically see him every Monday for the rest of the season. I am loath to part with my entry fee. Third, Graeme is still fun to hang out with. He has the same gregarious manner as Grant, and every night out with him is a virtual guarantee of meeting new women.

Graeme also misses having me around, so one night we make plans to meet at Mastro's steak house. Graeme has graduated from the B.W. to Mastro's because it is a higher energy place. There is a piano bar, and not surprisingly, he has gotten to know the piano player very well. His regular spot at the piano has replaced his usual corner-of-the-bar seat at the B.W, and he wants me to meet him there. We are to meet at 8:30, but I'm running a little bit late. I'm about ten minutes away when I get a call.

"Mike, where are you?"

"I'm on my way, Graeme."

"Hurry up," he says.

One of the things I recognize about myself is that I'm often in a hurry, especially when it comes to going out. If I'm late, I feel like I'm missing out on something. I inherited FOMO (fear of missing out) from my mother, but I have been making a conscious effort lately to relax and let things happen naturally.

I say, "Don't worry about it; I'll be there soon."

"No, you don't understand; I met somebody. Her name is Jody, and she lived in Denver when you were there. I can tell that we're just going to be friends, but I've been telling her about you. She wants to meet you, and wait until you hear who she used to go out with."

With Graeme's track record, I'm leery that he might be trying to line me up with a hooker. Nevertheless, I'm intrigued, so I put the heel to the steel. When I get there, Graeme has come through in a big way. I'm very jealous of his ability to start conversations with people. Jody had been the girlfriend of the Colorado Avalanche's best player in Denver at the same time that I was a season ticket holder. It immediately gives us something to talk about, although, she really doesn't even like hockey. She is originally from Texas and used go to the Avalanche games to get drunk in the executive suites. Nevertheless, she seems to like me, and I like women who like me.

Graeme was correct, she isn't interested in him in a sexual way, but she is interested in helping him sell his collectables. Before I got there, he must have told her about the hundreds of pounds of sports cards that he has accumulated. They start scheming about ways to sell his stuff on the Internet; she is going to broker the sales. It always comes down to some sort of a financial transaction for poor Graeme.

The evening progresses very well; Jody and I get along great, and we have a lot to talk about. Not only had we both lived in

Denver, but also we both recently moved to L.A. In spite of my weakness with social cues, I can tell there is chemistry here. The situation is complicated, however, by an agreement that Graeme has made with Jasmine earlier in the week. They decided to become exclusive – starting tomorrow. This allows each of them one last night to go out and have a final fling before they settle down. Of course, it is much easier for a woman to go out and have cheap sex than it is for a man. Given that Graeme has already been exclusively Jasmine's, and Jasmine is seeing God knows how many other guys, their agreement is very one-sided. As the evening progresses, Graeme becomes more and more desperate to find someone to fuck.

Graeme is addicted to his cell phone, especially texting. As he explains, texting is a great way to be social without actually being social. In fact, cell phones in general, and texting in particular, are annoyingly anti-social. For much of the time we are there, Graeme's eyes are riveted to his phone. He is completely detached from his current surroundings, but he can't stop because it is absolutely killing him that his girlfriend is out with someone else. He has fallen hard, and she now has the ability to completely dominate his thoughts with her actions. After about an hour, it is too much for him to take.

He finally pulls me aside and says, "I want to try and take Jody home tonight."

I understood his motivation; he is being completely emasculated by Jasmine and is desperate to try and regain his manhood. I try to be delicate because I can tell that he has no shot, "It's not really up to me, Graeme."

"I'm still going to try," he insisted.

"Fine, do whatever you want. Do you want me to leave?"

If he had said yes, I would have left, but he didn't want me to; instead, we all go over to the B.W. for a change of scenery. For the next hour, I feel like the third wheel. Graeme is coming on strong to Jody, and the only time that I get to talk to her is when he is distracted by another text from Jasmine, which fortunately is often. The whole situation is pathetic and I've had enough. I get up from our table and announce, "I'm going to take off."

And then Jody gives me the response I'm hoping for, "No, you should stay."

I sit back down, and wait to see if Graeme will get the message. He doesn't. For another hour, he keeps the full-court press on, and Jody is polite because she doesn't want to risk alienating a potential business partner.

As last call approaches, I finally say, "Graeme, we're leaving."

I feel bad about being so blunt, but was he not such an emotional wreck, he'd be happy for me. In a few days, he gets over it because he and his beloved Jasmine are now exclusive.

* * *

To celebrate their monogamy, Graeme takes Jasmine to Vegas the following weekend. While they're gone, I go back to the house to finish some work that he has asked me to do. The handyman has redone much of the woodwork on the patio trellis, and I have agreed to paint it. I am irritated with Graeme because I had asked him to let me paint the wood before it got put up, which would have been a hell of a lot easier. Nevertheless, I haven't done as much work as we had originally agreed, so I want to feel like I lived up to my end of the deal.

When I got there, Grant is dog sitting, which is only fair given that they are all his. As I paint, he sits outside by the pool smoking and talking on his cell phone. He is currently off-again with his former fiancée Lindsay, and is dating a new woman. I have seen this woman and am amazed. She is definitely hot, but Grant met her in rehab, so it's another damaged person. Regardless, Grant's luck with women is maddening. During the time I spent in the hospital, I didn't even meet a single woman that I would consider dating, let alone a good-looking one with big breasts.

He makes no attempt to lower his voice as he speaks, so I catch most of the conversation. Grant claims to be clean at this point, but much of the conversation revolves around drugs. I also hear him mention Jasmine several times in the context of drugs and money. I know exactly why she'd come up in the context of money, but I know nothing of her drug use.

When he gets off the phone, I ask, "What's that about Jasmine and drugs?"

"Apparently, she's a recreational drug user."

When Grant is speaking of drug use, you can safely substitute the word recreational with hard-core. Graeme has approached Grant to procure Demerol because Jasmine has a history of back-problems and needs relief. The obvious question is, *why not get a valid prescription from a doctor*? The obvious answer is, because no doctor of an ethical mind would ever prescribe Demerol for minor back pain. The situation is made more farcical by the fact that she isn't ever in too much pain to pass on sex.

I simply cannot conceive of the situation where my father would come to me and ask me to get him illegal prescription drugs for his girlfriend, but Grant seems to take it in stride. For the first time, I feel sorry for him having Graeme as a father rather than the other way around. Graeme's behavior is outrageous, and I wonder how often in the past Grant has had to tolerate his father's dysfunction.

The painting goes very slowly, and I don't complete it on the weekend. Back from Vegas, Graeme calls me to get together again. He doesn't seem to care that I haven't finished the painting and is extremely preoccupied when we speak. I'm still seeing Jody, but my last outing with Graeme went so well that I gladly agree to do it again. This time, however, Graeme implies that he has something serious he wants to talk to me about. I assume that it's mostly to do with his trip to Vegas and other things going on in his relationship, things he doesn't want to tell me over the phone. I'm happy to agree to the one-on-one talk because I enjoy every chance I get to tell him what a loser Jasmine is. We meet at the B.W. for a few cocktails.

The place is stone quiet, so we are able to focus on the conversation. After a few minutes of small talk, he starts talking about the thing that matters most to him—his relationship.

"Mike, I'm in trouble," he says in an almost cheery way.

"Why?" I ask, already knowing the answer but deciding to humor him anyway.

"I'm falling in love." Predictable. Aggravating.

"You've only known her for a month, so you can't be in love with her already. You're in love with..." He doesn't let me finish my sentence.

"I know, I know. I'm in love with being in love," and he says this with a proud smirk on his face.

"That's not what I was going to say. You're in love with the status of having a *10* on your arm," I say this as bluntly as I have ever said anything in my life. He finds this comment so distasteful that his face looks like I have just forced him to taste a large piece of the vilest shit ever produced.

"No." He shakes his head and that's all he'll hear of it. His reaction lets me know that I have hit his rawest nerve. To him, the cliché of being in love with being in love is cute, something that he can own up to without having to face the fact that his entire existence is about status. The truth hurts those who would rather ignore it.

He changes the topic to the details of his trip. He says they had a great time and that Jasmine has fallen in love with gambling, "She got addicted to it."

"Yeah, because she was probably playing with your money," I say.

No answer. Therefore the answer is yes.

"She told me something that really disappointed me, though," he mumbles this and looks down at his drink to avoid my eyes.

"What?"

"She sometimes works as an escort," he replies still not looking at me.

I've suspected as much from the beginning, but her plan has been well thought out. She didn't define herself as an escort when they met so that Graeme could see her as girlfriend material. Now that he is completely in love with her, she reveals it as a secondary part of her existence when, in fact, it defines her. Evidently, the plan works because Graeme chooses to say, *sometimes works as* instead of *she is*.

"We were in our hotel room stoned out of our minds, and we had this deep conversation about our lives. We shared our deepest secrets with each other," he says and his expression has changed. He is looking up and has a dreamy look on his face, like this was his most magical experience. He snuck stoned into the story – almost in passing – but I didn't miss it.

"What do you mean stoned? On what?"

"Coke," he replies without a hint of hesitation.

"What made you decide to do coke?"

"Well we were just sitting there in the hotel room, and she started unwrapping this little package of white powder. She asked me if I wanted some."

"You liked it?" I ask but know the answer.

"Oh yeah, it's the greatest drug ever invented," he looks sideways at me as he says this in a way that reminds me of a dirty old man leering at a nubile teenager.

"When people say that, it usually means that it's the worst drug ever invented. You need to be careful with that shit," I say very much speaking from experience.

Addictive personalities will latch onto anything that makes them feel good and do it until it no longer makes them feel good. It doesn't matter if it's drugs, sex, exercise, work, music, or golf.

I'm cursed with such a personality. Drugs are the most obviously dangerous addiction that I developed, but they are just a symptom of my personality. I have listened to my favorite song ten times in a row. I have obsessed about my golf swing until I have gotten so pissed-off that I didn't want to play anymore. I spent hundreds of hours developing the software for Second Wind because I couldn't relax until it was working properly.

I occasionally smoke pot – maybe once a year – but I am no longer interested in anything that I'll be tempted to use every day. Even before I got hooked on opiates, I remember watching an interview with Charlotte Caffey of *The Go-Go's*. She was talking about her heroin addiction and the damage it caused. She said that when she first tried it, she remembered thinking, "This is how I want to feel all the time."

I know that feeling, and now because of his whore, Graeme does too.

"Now you know where the $9000 went."

I have grown tired of asking him why he would still go out with her after he finds out this kind of thing, so I don't. It is obvious; he has no self-control whatsoever when it comes to this woman. She is addicted to painkillers and cocaine, and it takes her all of one weekend trip to get addicted to gambling. More troublesome, Graeme is beginning to alienate himself from important people in his life.

"Ryan and I had a big falling-out because he found the check," he says in a way that lets me know the discovery has made him extremely angry. His tone reminds me of a teenager who feels that his parents have no right to impose a curfew.

"I can't say I blame him for being pissed about you *lending* her nine grand," and I mean it.

"It's none of his business what I do with my money," he quickly shoots back.

"I thought that all the assets were in his name." It was hypocritical of Graeme to expect his son to play along with his financial games but then not have any input as Graeme pissed away the estate.

"I have my own money, and I can spend it however I want. I don't appreciate him invading my privacy," he says – again in a petulant manner.

I find his argument weak but know that he truly believes it, and I'm not going to be able to convince him otherwise. Everybody who cares about him is telling him to stop seeing this woman. He even reports to me what some of them say, like Stephanie who is apparently upset with him because he's dating such a young woman.

"She's a child!" is how Graeme told me she put it.

No Stephanie, I thought, this is anything but a child. This is the most cunningly evil adult I have ever met. She first identifies him as an easy mark, then she seduces him, and when his physical attraction to her may have waned because she revealed her career, she completes the trap with the cocaine.

Cunning is not to be mistaken with intelligence because she strikes me as a dullard. Rather, cunning is the ability to use a few simple tricks combined with the willingness to hurt others to get what you want. For most sociopaths, it is simply a matter of aping what has already been done to them. Perhaps Jasmine's pimp or dealer used her penchant for drugs to trap her, and she now feels entitled to deploy the strategy on Graeme. Whatever her thought process is, she doesn't give a flying fuck what happens to him while he still has money for her take.

After my evening out with Graeme, I call George to talk about the situation. I've never witnessed someone slide into destructive behavior like this, and I'm amazed at how far and fast Graeme is descending. I ask for George's advice on how to handle the situation, and his council is to completely disassociate from him. He tells me that Graeme is a loser and can only damage my image at USH. I disagree with him because I've already resolved to never let Graeme know where I work. If he meets my coworkers, he might find out that I lied to him about the Amgen job.

I also discount George's advice because I know that his motive is partly self-centered. Since George decided not to rent Graeme's townhouse, he has come over to hang out a couple of times. George is straight, but he can be confused for a gay man. If someone jokes about that in any way, they quickly become enemies. A number of times Graeme has made cutting, marginally funny comments about George being a homo. Following his usual pattern, George's doesn't say anything at the time, but then absolutely seethes later. He is so defensive and pissed off by Graeme's gay jokes, that he wants everybody he knows to punish him. Because I know this, plus the fact that I don't abandon friends who have helped me, I decide not to completely cut things off. I do take George's comments as an extra reason to be cautious, so I will continue to keep Graeme away from my professional life and see him only in public settings.

CHAPTER 11 – ENTOURAGE

By the end of October, Graeme's priorities have drastically changed, and he is no longer coming to hockey. During the summer season, I always knew I could find out what time we played from Graeme, but now, he is calling me for the times. When he does, I assume that means he is going to play, but lately he changes his mind by game-time. It's never a huge surprise to me when he doesn't show up because 90% of the times I talk to him, he sounds terrible. I worry that he's going to end up in hospital soon. Curiously though, the few times he doesn't sound horrible, he sounds fantastic. There is no in-between, but one thing for sure—he seldom sounds like the guy I became friends with six months ago. I am pretty certain that he was using *the greatest drug ever invented* every day.

I've never asked him if he is missing his hockey team, but we definitely are missing him. Jay, a comedian, has gone back to Canada to tour, and several other players have quit coming on a regular basis. A fully engaged Graeme would have found a replacement for Jay and called the whole team on game-day to make sure that we had a full roster. Without this direction, we are routinely playing with six or seven skaters and have lost four games in a row, after a 3-0 start. Things will likely get much worse for us if Graeme's active involvement with the team is finished.

Partying has replaced hockey as priority number one. He is infatuated, not only with Jasmine but also with the world she lives in. For the six months that I've known him, his circle of friends have been made up primarily of wheat-fed, prairie-born hockey players from Canada. There are a few Americans sprinkled in, but to a man, his friends look like Wonder Bread with the crusts cut off. Steadily and very quickly he has replaced his white friends with black friends. This wouldn't be a bad thing except that they are the type of people who associate with escorts, the type of people who know a meal ticket when they see one. Gooch replaced me; Sean "The Blur" replaced James, and so on down the list. He is completely enamored of his new clique and constantly raves about them and what great, exciting people they are. I know very well that The Blur was a former Seattle Seahawk because Graeme has told me that as many times as he has told me the Gretzky story.

George comments derisively, "He just likes to make himself feel cool by surrounding himself with good athletes."

This is a true statement because you can tell a lot about a person by those they choose to spend time with. These new athletes are a long way from the small-town hockey players of Graeme's past. They are gangsta rapper-types who think that toting guns is the thing to do – minor league versions of Michael Vick, Maurice Clarett, or Pacman Jones. Cocaine, testosterone, hookers, and guns are an explosive combination, which all of us who genuinely care about Graeme can see. He not only ignores the danger but also makes it worse with his open-door policy. Every time I go to Graeme's house to drop off or pick up Sherwood, there is someone hanging out on the couch. Maybe they are harmless, but I know these people are friends of Jasmine's and that makes me nervous.

Going to Graeme's reminds me of the feeling I get when hiking in bear country; I make as much noise as possible when I enter the house so as not to surprise anyone. I know that Graeme thrives on drama, but I can't imagine anyone being comfortable living in that environment.

There are losers in every race, but he would not have gotten mixed up with white, meth-addicted trailer trash because it isn't cool. That black thugs are somehow more compelling and glamorous is an insane notion caused by the rap culture permeating America. It has become far worse than the glorification of Italian Mafia because anyone can participate. Buy a gun; smoke some crack, you're in.

One of the leading figures in this culture is Marion "Suge" Knight, founder of Death Row Records. He also happens to be one of Jasmine's boyfriends, and allegedly the one who has caused her back problems. Jasmine claims that he knocked her around and damaged her back, thus the need for copious amounts of painkillers. This explanation seems a little too convenient, but at the same time it's believable. Having seen the way she manipulates Graeme, I can imagine how a gigantic, street-savvy man would react to her conniving strategies. Likely, Suge rather than Graeme is Jasmine's primary target, but he has survived way too much to be taken down by her. Graeme is the easy score to tide her over while she fantasizes about living in the big leagues.

"She's hoping that he'll marry her," Graeme confides to me over the phone.

"She's dreaming," I immediately respond.

There could be a hundred other women with the same misguided dream. Graeme agrees, and this is the reason that her infatuation with Suge Knight doesn't bother him. Of course, there is absolutely nothing he could do if it did, but still his comfort is in knowing that she is mostly a pretty little sex toy to Suge. This is probably the only instance in which Graeme can see a situation more clearly than Jasmine. Unfortunately, he won't acknowledge that having this convicted felon as a part of the equation is exceptionally dangerous. Graeme seems to care more about having another name to drop than admitting to the obvious danger he's in with his association with Jasmine's crowd.

I have never once held back about what I think of his new entourage and once said to him, "I'll go out with you, but we're going to play in my sandbox, not yours."

Based on his expression, my stance didn't seem to bother him. I'm sure that he considers it my loss not his, but making it clear to Graeme that I wouldn't associate with these people is my only option. Obviously, I know that these people aren't safe, but, more importantly, I've learned an important lesson from my marriage. I'll now only be around people whose company I enjoy. In fact, by far the best part of being divorced from Sandra is that I no longer had to tolerate her friends.

Soon after we moved to Raleigh, Sandra met a woman with whom she quickly formed a codependent relationship. Within three months of meeting, they were referring to each other as *sisters*. This would have been fine except that a husband came attached to her new sister. He resembles a penis with ears, so one could describe him as a prick, but that would be giving him too much credit. Rather, he's the waste of skin attached to a prick.

Mr. Foreskin and I happened to work at the same company where he was a middle-management stooge. I was made well aware of his job title and six-figure salary within the first five minutes of meeting him. He too is Canadian, but he doesn't deserve the citizenship. He doesn't like hockey, and if he watches, he cheers for Boston. We began to clash very quickly because he expected that I would be submissive to him. He can only see the world in terms of his job, so intelligence, education, and athletic ability are irrelevant to him. He possesses none of these things, yet he saw me as a lowly contractor, so beneath him in his little world. This method of ranking helped him to compensate for his impotence at home. He was exceedingly subservient to his wife, and it bothered him greatly that I wasn't to Sandra. He began to hate me to the extent that he undermined our marriage every chance he got. Sandra admitted to me after our divorce that when we would bicker in front of them he would shoot her looks as if to say, *"How much longer are you going to put up with this?*

One time, Foreskin and I were talking about Canada and the possibility of ever moving back home. The conversation moved to the topic of foreign exchange rate, and he commented how happy he was to be making the big Yankee bucks. He was certain he'd be much better off in the long run with a portfolio made up entirely of American investments. At the time, the Canadian dollar was at near record lows against the American currency, and I remembered a couple things my dad told me about investing. It is very difficult not to let current conditions bias your forecast, but diversification is always a good strategy. Applying that to the current conversation, I suggested that he might actually consider diversifying his portfolio with Canadian investments, particularly since he had the legal right to live in either country. He seemed shocked that I could be so stupid, and pitied me because I actually thought that the currency markets might shift in favor of the Canadian dollar.

I was simply trying to give Foreskin another perspective when thinking about his investments. He rejected my advice in a condescending way, but in the long run, it turned out great for me. Any money he would have moved into Canadian investments would have returned 50% from the currency shifts alone; however, the knowledge that Foreskin missed out on a big return because of his arrogance and stupidity was little consolation. Sandra wouldn't accept that I didn't want him around me, and this played a critical role in the demise of our marriage. Initially, I tried to play nice, but his egotism was just too grating. When I told her time and again that I didn't want them around me, Sandra responded by saying, “If you can’t get along with my friends, we’re going to have a problem.”

My frustration was compounded by her insistence that every holiday, vacation or other special event had to involve her friends. Before long, her friends consisted exclusively of people who were also friends of Foreskin and his wife. They claimed to love our children, but obviously not as much as they hated me. It enraged me that they weren’t willing to back away and instead chose to constantly interfere. In my opinion, if you aren’t willing to help two people stay married, at least get the hell out of the way and don’t make the situation worse. Unless you are incredibly selfish, friendship should take a distance backseat to maintaining the integrity of a family. You back away for the sake of the children.

Escaping this impossible situation with Hydrocodone wasn’t the answer, and I’ll live with that mistake for the rest of my life. It’s easy now to see that I should have insisted that those people were not welcome in my house because then we might still have a family. The question is, can a man do that anymore without being labeled an abuser? One certainly walks a fine line, but in this case I think my insistence would have been justified.

Her friends made it known that they felt I wasn’t worthy of Sandra, and their selfish goals became obvious shortly after our split. They set her up with a new boyfriend, and she has been aggressively forming a stepfamily with this new man ever since. She chooses to believe that he is Mr. Right, which is convenient because he fits in perfectly with their group.

Being pushed out of my family and replaced by someone who could get along with her friends was demoralizing. For some reason, it had been my worst fear all along. Perhaps I sensed something, or maybe my own insecurities became self-fulfilling. I had lost a battle with someone who had no business fighting in the first place. The damage was lessened somewhat by the knowledge that Sandra's need to replace me immediately is not unique.

Shortly after the divorce, I wound up on the other side of the equation when I dated a single mom. She introduced me to her children on our third date, and they were about the same age as my kids. It disturbed me that she had brought her children along; I had made it very clear that I was recently divorced and it was too soon for a committed relationship. In spite of my honesty, she held out hope that we *could have so much more* than just dating. Self-deception allowed to her to immediately insert her children into the mix. Her son was still a little too young to form any type of opinion about me, but her daughter looked at me with a fearful trepidation that I suspected came from having been down this road before. It was very sad to see that look from a six-year-old, and there is no one to blame but her mother for the pattern that she will likely repeat someday.

Two of my best friends in Los Angeles, James and Dave, both had fathers who divorced their mothers and moved away when they were young. Their mothers remarried, and we've talked about how this affected them. While they are philosophical about it now, not having their dads around left a permanent mark on them. I think about that in relation to my son and me. Every time I say goodbye to Johnathan after a visit, he cries heart-wrenching tears. The divorce has left a permanent mark on him, and that angers me.

The planet is full of sociopaths who damage other people in ways that are malicious but not technically illegal. These same people then rely on society to protect them from the consequences. That's a flaw in our system. If Jasmine hadn't introduced Graeme to cocaine, everything she did would have been perfectly legal. Foreskin acted immorally, yet I have no legal recourse against him. I imagine somewhere, sometime, fixing my own particular instance of the flaw. As Foreskin is lying on his back looking up at me, trying to see me in spite of his shattered nose, I will make it clear that he should have kept it out of my marriage. He will feel wrath brought on by the misery of seeing my son's bitter tears, and I hope when it happens his son is there to hear me say, “This is what happens when you fuck with me. Tell your friends.”

Occasionally, Graeme and I talk about the circumstances of my separation and the disagreements that Sandra and I have had. In much the same way George has done, he advises me to be as civil as possible. Unlike George, who can sometimes have trouble following his own sound counsel, Graeme was seemingly very gracious in dividing assets with his ex-wife. He claims that things have turned out better in the long run because he essentially gave her everything and started over. Graeme believes it is most important to keep things friendly, rather than fight. That attitude definitely fits in with his pattern of dealing with women, so his position doesn’t surprise me. I think, however, that he has been extremely lucky that things turned out so well for him – perhaps too lucky for the story to be entirely true.

My next trip to see the kids is in early November, and I am far from ready to be a doormat for Sandra. We have another fight because, while with me, Johnathan lost his autographed Carolina Hurricanes jersey. Sandra had stood in line for hours after the ‘Canes won the Stanley Cup to get it autographed. I take no joy that the jersey is lost, but I also feel that Jonathon is getting old enough to take care of his favorite possessions. Sandra disagrees, and even though the jersey is later recovered, it remains a point of contention. I am also annoyed because the kids have more stories about the budding new stepfamily. Fortunately, dating a woman with a porn star body temporarily makes Sandra's situation seem somewhat less important. Nevertheless, I feel that Sandra's dating choices are impulsive, neurotic, passive-aggressive, damaging, selfish, and a few other things too.

I hate saying goodbye to the kids, but as always, I am happy to get the hell out of Raleigh. Still too many memories there. When I get back to L.A, I have to pick up Sherwood, so I stop for a few minutes to visit Graeme. The only member of the family maintaining a grip on sanity is Ryan, and he also happens to be at the house. I have only actually seen him in person three or four times, but each time his attitude towards me has been frosty. I'm pretty sure that he viewed me as a freeloader and questioned his father's impulsive decision to invite me to live there. This time, however, he is unequivocally pleasant. It appears that he has gotten past any resentment or suspicion because I have lived up to my commitments, and more importantly, I'm not Jasmine. Graeme is still trying to salvage his relationship with this son, so they are in family counseling. Perhaps, it has come out in session that I have been warning Graeme not to give Jasmine money and Ryan realizes that we are on the same side. Whatever the case, he stays to visit for a few minutes.

When Ryan leaves, the conversation turns to women. I listen patiently to more stories about Jasmine and their latest exploits. She has recently managed to piss-off Wolfgang Puck in his new B.W restaurant, Cut. Wolfgang sat down at their table to visit and Jasmine proceeded to get *a little rambunctious.* Her behavior was so boorish that Graeme feels he can no longer go back there when Wolfgang is around. On another expensive dinner date, Graeme had bonded with Larry David from across Mastro's by slicking his hand on top of his bald head. Larry gave him a big thumbs-up, probably hoping that would be good enough for the lunatic with the hooker.

Graeme is starting to look like a lunatic. Given that he is eating out all the time and not showing up for hockey, his noticeable weight loss isn't due to diet and exercise. He is quite happy with the transformation, but his hair appears brittle and his eyes are starting to bug out of their sockets. His personality hasn't yet completely altered, so he is still curious about the goings-on in my life.

"What about you and Jody?" he asks.

"Fine, it's not a long-term thing. She still wants to sell your stuff," I say.

I know I'm not going to be dating her for much longer, because I've seen another side of her personality. After our first night together, she asked for my number, in case she needed a booty call. At first this was a pretty good deal for me, but I soon learned she could be sweet and nice one moment and then turn nasty with minimal provocation. I have the feeling that it will only be a matter of time before she pisses me off enough not to talk to her again, but for now I'm trying to be a friend. Her BMW has recently been repossessed, she is having trouble finding a job, and she has moved into a tiny one-bedroom apartment with a roommate. Clearly, her finances have seen better days, so I am happy to be intermediary between her and Graeme. In Denver, she became part owner of a restaurant by hard work and personality, and I believe she will eventually hustle her way out of her current predicament.

Selling Graeme's collectables is part of her plan, and he is eager to participate. In spite of the drugs, his helpful nature still dominates his personality, but he is also probably interested in the quid pro quo aspect of the deal. He is burning through money at a pace that would ruin almost anybody. He confesses that he bought Jasmine a $2000 dog and co-signed for a new car. Cocaine isn't cheap, either. I plead with him to dump her and never call her again because he has, from my estimate, blown about $50K on her in three months. His current lifestyle isn't sustainable, and his world is crumbling. It isn't too late to turn that around, but he needs to make changes quickly.

CHAPTER 12 – "GRAEME'S GONNA DIE."

Maybe life is really a zero-sum game; one man's ascent from the depths of despair is another's decline. Perhaps, that's a pessimistic way of looking at the world, but there are no winners without losers. You don't really score a goal if you're not scoring on someone. A good compromise usually means everyone is unhappy. Many would argue that the competition that creates winners and loser propels us all to greater heights than we could otherwise reach. This may be true in the big picture, but in my little corner of the world, Graeme is declining at least as quickly as I am recovering.

The month of November is when USH does its annual budgeting, and the process is completely new to me. On top of that, we are short staffed, so I'm working 70-hour weeks. I'm busting hard to impress my bosses and am succeeding at it. Conversely, I haven't heard Graeme talk about any type of work since he testified as an expert witness in a construction dispute

– his last paid visit to a courtroom. The only work Graeme's focusing on is trying to hold on to Jasmine who has now begun the final phase of her manipulation plan—the breakup. Now that he is completely dependent upon her, she has begun demonstrating her dominance in the relationship by letting him know that he is disposable.

"Jasmine and I are finished," he declares to me one day.

"Really? Well that's good," I say completely relieved and happy for him. "You needed to break away from her. What made you finally decide to get rid of her?"

"I didn't appreciate her giving one of my friends a blowjob in the bathroom of my house," he says.

Sandra had used sex as a weapon against me, but this is a nuclear warhead compared to anything she ever did. As if the bathroom blowjob isn't bad enough, Jasmine has also tried to get something started with Grant. After he moved to Thousand Oaks with his fiancée/girlfriend/ex, whatever she was at the time, things got ugly. With me out of the house he has been crashing in his old bedroom a lot. Jasmine told Graeme soon after she started dating him that she thought Grant was hot. One evening he was in his bedroom, and Jasmine walked in and started kissing him. I don't know how much further it got, but Grant is not exactly a tower of self-discipline. Finally, her disgusting behavior made Graeme realize she wasn't the greatest thing that ever happened to him.

* * *

Now that he's no longer seeing Jasmine, I hope that Graeme will regain his passion for hockey. The team needs him; we have lost seven games in a row.

"Are you going to hockey tonight?"

"I don't think I can make it," he says, and he sounds like shit.

"Why not?"

"I'm helping Jasmine get moved into her new apartment," he says like we had never had the conversation about their breakup. She obviously fucked Graeme just in time for him to help her move. Big surprise. Thus starts a pattern that I can see will continue as long as it suits her—they won't officially be together anymore unless she wants something.

By the time I get off the phone, I'm aghast at how feeble Graeme sounds. In my mind, I start a countdown to his death. That's a helpless, morbid feeling, and I feel guilty, but all my instincts are telling me he's a dead man walking. Even before this call, James and I have spoken at length about Graeme's spiral, but we don't have any good ideas about how to deal with the situation.

The next day I decide to call Jody and see if she has any thoughts, "Do you want to get together? I've got something I want to talk to you about."

"What is it?" she snaps.

"I don't want to talk about it over the phone," I say.

"Just spit it out." Uh oh. The ugly side of Jody seems to be in full control.

"It's not really a phone conversation," I insist. We argued for a couple of minutes over whether I should tell her now or in-person. I can tell that she has very little patience for me this moment, so I give in and begin to tell the story. "I just thought you might be interested to know that your potential business partner is using coke, big time. I'm trying to figure out what to do."

"There's nothing interesting about that. We don't need to get together for that," she says.

"Fine." I said matter-of-factly.

I'm about to hang up when she softens slightly, "You go over there and you don't leave his house until he agrees to go to rehab. I know. I've had lots of experience with this."

Ah, I knew it! That's why I called her about this in the first place. I have seen pictures in her apartment taken backstage with Van Halen and others. I suspected that she would have insight, but she doesn't need to be such a bitch about it.

"What if he refuses?" I'm hopeful that she'll have a good answer for this question because it's a key one.

"You make him."

"How do I make him go? He's a lawyer and he knows his rights. I can't make him do anything," I insist. I speculate that Jody has likely never tried her brilliant strategy on someone like Graeme. Not only that, he doesn't feel that he has a problem.

"You put a bag over his head and tie him up if you have to. If you're his friend you'll make him go. Be a man," she baits.

Lately, this ugly side of her personality has dominated our interactions, and I don't appreciate her tone or overly simplistic advice. I recognize her pattern— a person pushes you right up to the edge of what you will tolerate, and then backs off just enough to keep you around. This highlights another reason I'm so aggravated by my divorce; dating sucks. I loathe the idea of having to come out of the comfortable built-in date of marriage to navigate the world of the needy, manic-depressives, and psychotics. I've had enough, so I politely thank her for her advice and say goodbye. That's the end of Jody in my life.

A few days later, I get a text from her asking me how I'm doing as if nothing has happened. Maybe from her perspective nothing has happened, but I delete it and hope I never hear from her again. If I don't take my own advice, why should Graeme?

Meanwhile, Jasmine's drug use is having some serious consequences for Graeme, which is really not a surprise.

"Suge called me," Graeme confides.

"Why would he call you?" I ask. I'm incredulous that a little pip like Graeme would be on Suge Knight's radar, but Graeme seems determined to make his life as dramatic and dangerous as possible.

"He wanted to get together to talk about Jasmine." Big uh oh. There can be nothing good coming out of a conversation like that.

"You didn't go did you?" I ask.

"Yeah, I did."

"What's the problem? Did he want you to stop seeing her?"

"Well, when I got there he put his gun on the table, so I knew he was serious. Basically, he told me to stop enabling her habits," he explains. Graeme has been giving her so much money that she has the resources to do whatever she wants. Before Graeme, if she wanted some cocaine, she had to pay for it or sleep with her dealer. Now, she is mixing the dangerous combination of painkillers and cocaine with impunity, basically a hillbilly speedball.

"I thought he weighed 400lbs. Does he really need to threaten you with a gun? What a coward."

"No, I think he just wanted me to understand that he was serious. He's actually a really nice guy."

"He sounds like it," I say heavy on the sarcasm. "What's going on with her?"

"She's been having convulsions. A couple of times I've had to hold her down right in the middle of my living room until they pass," he says in a way that completely minimized the situation.

"Holy Fuck, Graeme!"

"It's not that big a deal. I've been through this type of thing before, but Suge's not happy. Her problem is that she can't control herself the way I can, so Suge and I are going to get her the help she needs."

I am immediately reminded of Vanilla Ice's story of near-death at the hands of Mr. Suge Knight. I've seen him on VH1 claiming that he was held upside down by his ankles from the balcony of a top floor hotel room. Vanilla later admitted that Suge had not done this and was simply, "firm but nice." Perhaps he had been gun-on-the-table firm.

If Suge Knight gave a fuck about what happens to Graeme, he would have told Graeme to get his ass into rehab as well, but he doesn't. Whether Graeme lives or dies is irrelevant as long as Jasmine is taken care of. It is a very strange dynamic that he cares enough about her to threaten Graeme's life, but if she has regular sex with him that's OK. Likely, Suge has enough women that it doesn't bother him. Any thoughts I might have had about trying the tough-love approach with Graeme disappear after I hear this story. In fact, James and I start making unfortunate jokes at Jody's expense. I call him up and say, "Yeah, James, why don't you go over to Graeme's today and take him to rehab. Be a man."

We are making light of a very serious situation, but it bothers us that we can't do anything to get Graeme out of his destructive spiral. Trying to execute any plan for rescue would be fraught with danger. With all the scum hanging out at Graeme's, we wouldn't know what kind of hornet's nest we'd be walking into. If those people got the sense that we were cutting off their gravy train, we'd be in trouble. And make no mistake Graeme is a gravy train. In spite of Jody's questioning my friendship with Graeme, I feel that I'm being the best friend that I can without risking my own safety.

On one hand, I don't want to be like the women in his life who used him for whatever they can get, giving little back in return. On the other, Graeme understands his rights as well as anyone. If he doesn't want to go to rehab, nobody is going to make him. Forcing someone to go where he doesn't want to go is either kidnapping or arrest. Since I'm not a cop, I would fall in the category of kidnapper.

I think about maybe trying to get a few people together to form an intervention, but I don't have the phone numbers for anyone he might listen to. The best person to call would be Ryan, but if I ask for that number, Graeme will be suspicious immediately. I'm also not sure if Ryan would have any interest.

I resolve to keep talking sense into Graeme every time I see him, and I'll keep the rest of the team informed about his spiral, with the hope that they'll do the same. On the Monday night that turns out to be our ninth loss in a row, Jason is sitting next to me, and I'm giving him the most recent information.

"What's this?" one of the other guys asks from across the room, "what about Graeme?"

"Graeme's gonna die!" Jason says.

Much like Ryan's "Dad, she's black," comment, three words say everything.

Jason realizes, as I do, that Graeme knows the consequences of his behavior, doesn't care, and doesn't want help. On many, many occasions he prophetically proclaims, "I'm having the time of my life!"

It's true. This time in his life will forever define him.

My busy schedule continues through the Thanksgiving weekend, which Graeme spends with Jasmine and her mother. When I ask about his celebration, he doesn't mention his sons, and I don't see or hear from him again until the third week in

December when our mutual friend, Anthony, comes back into town. I haven't talked to Anthony since the summer because he's been out east playing NCAA Division I hockey. Of course, Graeme immediately buys his friendship by hiring him to do various menial tasks around his office. Even though I'm certain Graeme hasn't had any client business lately, he still feels that he needs Anthony on the payroll. He has moved his law office into his house, and is finally getting around to fully cleaning out the townhouse office.

Anthony is fun to skate with, but I don't know him that well away from the rink. We decide to go to Graeme's new Beverly Hills hangout, Aqua. I meet them at the house because they are going to be back and forth to the townhouse all day. When I get there, Grant has a friend over. As introductions are made, they are so obviously stoned that I'm somewhat taken aback. The entire time I've known Grant, he has been either momentarily clean, in rehab, or pretending to be clean. This time, he is feeling no pain, and both of them exude a relaxation and good nature that is certainly drug-induced. Grant is sweating a bit from the intensity of the high, and even a punch to the face probably couldn't have gotten his attention.

I guess they are using heroin and later tell Graeme of my suspicions, but he dismisses them, "He's not doing heroin."

"How do you know that?" I challenge.

"Because I talked to his dealer myself," he says without blinking.

"You know his dealer?"

"Yeah. I asked him not to sell him anything but pot," Graeme says, as he secures his father-of-the-year nomination. He knows Grant's dealer personally.

"You don't seriously believe him?" I ask.

"Yes. He promised me."

Oh, OK. Now I can understand Graeme's confidence because a drug dealer's word is his bond.

"You don't get like he is from smoking pot. He's doing something stronger," I insist, but Graeme will not be convinced otherwise. He chooses to believe that Grant is only using pot because it makes the situation easier for him. If he acknowledges that Grant is using highly dangerous drugs, he might have to face the fact that he is responsible for his son's destruction. At least this way he can temporarily avoid reality.

This is when Graeme ceases to be a father in my mind. Fathers don't choose hookers over their kids. Fathers don't ask dealers to sell their kid only pot. If they have to, fathers hunt down drug dealers, chase them through several rooms, and then kill them. Of course, for what Grant is going to go through, it will probably be best to be completely numb.

In spite of my dismay with Graeme, I go out with them to the bar, but spend most of the night talking with Anthony. Graeme isn't really interested in talking to me anyway because he's there to network and find the next great business idea. He divulges that he already has several ideas in the planning stage, and if any one of them hit, it is going to be huge. Delusion has set in.

Aqua isn't what I imagined but should have; it has mostly an upscale black crowd. While Anthony and I discuss the state of college hockey, Graeme spends the evening as a social butterfly bouncing from conversation to conversation trying to be the hip, old dude. He has also gotten in the habit of carrying a hanky around with him and is constantly dabbing at his nose.

"Did you see that score I just made?" he asks after returning to where Anthony and I are standing.

"What score?" I ask even though I have just seen a truly beautiful black girl humoring him, and I assume that is what he's talking about.

"That woman I was just talking to wants to be a lawyer. I'm in like Flynn baby!" In reality he has no shot, but I get his point.

After not getting much of a reaction from me, he takes off again. Eventually, I notice him settle into a conversation with a group of three people: two well-dressed, middle-aged black guys and their young blond companion. I keep an eye on them and notice that Graeme is completely rapt by the conversation, which seems to last about an hour. When he comes back over to us, he tells me that he has just stumbled onto something huge. He can't believe his luck, and he wants to meet with me the next day. He is going to put together the deal for a new construction material that his new friends have the rights to. He wants my help putting together an initial business plan.

"Sure. What time?" I offer. The last thing I want to do is work on a business plan on my weekend, but I agree anyhow. For one thing, he is about to let me leave Sherwood at the house while I take my kids to Canada for a week over the Christmas holiday. I am also curious, skeptical, but curious nonetheless, as to what this *huge* new building material is.

By this time, Anthony has gotten drunk and is telling us how pissed off he is at his girlfriend back at school. He wants to get laid, and he wants Graeme to help get him hooked up. Maybe Graeme has told Anthony the story of Jody, but that type of lightning in a bottle only happens occasionally. Tonight, they will have to settle for hookers and blow. I'm not interested in paying for a hooker, nor am I interested in having Graeme pay for one for me, but Anthony has no such scruples. He did help Graeme move, after all.

When Graeme ran the hockey team, he had a strict policy about not offering scholarships to good players he wanted to entice onto his team. He reasons that if they really wanted to play, they would be willing to pay. If they weren't, why should Graeme pay the $400 for their season? I agree completely, but because of this policy he has had to put up with some players he really didn't want on the team. Now, Graeme is about to drop $400 for one night with a hooker, and the amount of money he is spending in one weekend would have been enough to pay the whole hockey team for an entire season.

I leave them to their business and call Graeme the next day to figure out when we are getting together. No answer. I send him a text message asking him if he still wants to get together.

I get a quick response, "Not today," and that's the end of it.

When I drop Sherwood off before my Christmas trip later that week, he doesn't mention anything about his new business opportunity, so I don't either. While I do hear several times over the next couple of months just how huge this new material is going to be, he never again asks me to put together a business plan for him.

* * *

Back when the Oilers were a dynasty, we got really spoiled by the quality of the hockey played by Gretzky, Messier, Coffey and the rest. I remember reading an article in the local paper after a game that didn't live up to expectations. The columnist wrote that it had been, "about as exciting as winter in Weyburn."

The Weyburn to which he had been referring was in the middle of the bald Saskatchewan prairie, and it also happened to be my mom's hometown. Well, I'm spending my Christmas in Weyburn with the rest of my family, and it is fantastic. We have 30 cousins from five families with three generations well represented. We are all staying under one roof at my aunt and uncle's farm, and it is one of those memories-to-last-a-lifetime Christmases. Kyndal and Johnathan have played non-stop with their cousins, and I've enjoyed being a single-dad. This is one of the times I feel like they are as much my kids as they are Sandra's. They go long periods without even mentioning Sandra, and when she does call, they are having too much fun to talk to her very long.

A couple times, my family ask me where Sherwood is while I'm on holidays, and I tell them, "At my friend Graeme's."

I don't dare tell them the whole story, but mentioning him causes me to start wondering how he is spending Christmas. He's going down a tragic path, and I doubt the holidays will do anything to keep him from destroying himself.

CHAPTER 13 – CONFINEMENT AND OBLIVION

One evening after I moved into my apartment, I took Sherwood out for his twice-daily walk. Living in an apartment meant that I no longer had the benefit of the dog doors and gardeners that were so convenient at Graeme's place. I happened to cross paths with a neighbor, who was coming inside with his dog as I was leaving the building. His dog managed to pull off of his leash and the dogs immediately began fighting. I was trapped up against the building and had nowhere to go, so I held tight on Sherwood and waited for the neighbor to pull his dog back. He didn't; he just stood there and watched, until his dog started to lose. Then, he got between the dogs and started kicking and pulling on Sherwood. Finally, the dogs stopped fighting, but now it was our turn.

"Dude! You are a fucking idiot," he screamed.

He proceeded to unleash a verbal attack on me for not pulling my dog away. Very quickly, I began to return the obscenities, and told him that if his dog hadn't been loose there wouldn't have been a problem. It was clear, though, that he wasn't going to admit fault, even though his dog was off leash. After a couple more minutes, I wasn't willing to waste any more time with him, so I called him a fucking idiot one last time and walked away. He, however, wasn't done and said something else to me as I tried to walk away. I don't remember exactly what he said to make me turn back around, but it was a threat. I walked back toward him with one thing on my mind; I was ready to go. I stopped and stood five feet in front of him while he resumed his verbal assault. He tried to goad me back into the argument, but I simply stood there silently, prepared. He sensed that his words were having no further effect on me, and it frustrated him.

"Are you just going to stand there like an idiot?" He raged.

"I'm done talking," I was seething with a rage of my own, and there was only one thing left to do.

I heard his wife say, "He just wants to stare you down."

She couldn't have been more wrong. I wanted to hurt him, but I wasn't going to start it. I stood there silently, with my focus on his jaw so that the second he made a move towards me, I was ready to break it. As I waited for him to decide what he would do, I was confident that my posture left him with two options: throw down or leave me alone. I forgot that assholes are unpredictable when their bluff is called, and he managed to come up with a third option.

“Oh yeah, well what would you do if I sprayed you with this,” he said as he pulled something from his jacket. I didn’t move and watched as he put his finger on the button and moved the mace canister to within six inches of my eyes. It was one of those situations in life when you’re amazed by the behavior of another.

“I’d sue you,” I said as I turned my back on him and walked away, finally able to take Sherwood for his walk.

When I got back to my apartment, Mace Boy had cooled off enough to apologize but in a way only a true jerk-off could. He said that I had frozen up, the whole thing was my fault, but he was willing to let it go if I was. I wasn’t, but I didn’t want to deal with him anymore and said, “Whatever.”

I needed to get away from him. I went into my apartment feeling a mix of anger and sadness. The anger was because this neighbor had been at once hyper-aggressive and gutless. I would spend the next few months hoping he would have the nerve to come out from behind his weapon. The sadness was because I still seemed to lack the ability to get along with people.

I sat down on the couch and began to stew about what had just happened when I heard a knock at my door. I opened the door, I expected to see Mace Boy again, but instead I was very surprised to meet a female neighbor whom I had never even seen before. She introduced herself and proceeded to explain that she had seen the whole incident. She assured me that I had done everything right, and she was amazed that I was able to keep my composure. She let me know that I wasn't the first person to have problems with that neighbor, and that she would fully support me in whatever action I wanted to take. I was fairly certain that pulling mace on me without provocation was a serious assault, and I certainly would have liked to see him spend some time in jail.

Because I had an eyewitness, I filed a complaint with the management of the apartment building the next day. He received a written reprimand, and over the next couple of days, I debated the merit of filing a police report. Ultimately, I decided against it because I knew that even when you're in the right, cops have a way of making you feel like a suspect. I didn't want to make the Los Angeles police aware of my presence because I was fairly certain that, in Raleigh, I had been put in the category of "known to police". I also knew that my name would go into the L.A.P.D database, and that is certainly not an organization that inspires confidence. I had no interest in seeing if they could find a way to turn the situation into my fault.

My next instinct was to wait for the right time, and beat the hell out of him before he could get his finger on the button. It was reasonable for me to be furious, but George has a saying I agree with, "Don't make yourself look like the problem."

By assaulting him, I would have turned the whole situation around, and I would have looked like the criminal. Doing the right thing in this case was extremely difficult, but George's advice still resonated. I also sucked up my pride because the nightmare of incarceration was fresh in my mind. I have never been charged with a crime let alone convicted of one, but I discovered that crime is not the only way to find your freedoms taken away. My time in a cage, brief as it was, provided with me new perspective on the minor aggravations of life.

Eventually the neighbor and I reached a truce. We're certainly not buddies, but at least we're civil, largely because I'm able to control my temper. He may have even reached the conclusion that the situation is actually his fault and he's very lucky that I didn't call the police. That's doubtful, but possible. Regardless, I'm happy with the way I handled the entire episode, especially since Sandra used to say many times when she was describing me, "He's got anger issues."

I was shamed by her words because that was how she had described every single one of her prior boyfriends. I absolutely didn't want to be lumped in with them and had spent our entire marriage trying to suppress my aggressive nature.

More and more women are discovering that an effective, incontestable way of lashing out at men is to label them *verbally abusive.* Sandra leveled this allegation against me even though only she, on two separate occasions, resorted to physical violence. She didn't have the strength to actually hurt me, but it was behavior that I would never have tolerated from a man. Moreover, if I had done the same thing to her, she would have called the police immediately. Sandra was the one common denominator in each of her abusive relationships, and my guess is that anyone involved with her could easily have anger issues. Not necessarily because she is attracted exclusively to flawed men, but rather because she makes people angry. This is a very effective, perhaps unintentional, manipulation technique that I didn't recognize at the time.

Growing up, I went to church regularly and was taught to believe that anger and similar heated emotions are proof that we are imperfect beings. I then wondered how God can be considered to be perfect when he is repeatedly described in parts of the Bible as angry and vengeful. The answers that I got to these questions were less than satisfactory, so I eventually considered myself agnostic. Now, I look at the world in terms of evolution and try to understand why the emotions we all possess have been genetically persistent. Aggressive males and selective females is a mating dynamic common to most species. In humans, females usually base their selectivity largely on relative wealth. It is commonplace in Los Angeles, where many of the super-rich reside, to see fat, ugly guys with drop-dead gorgeous women, and that's not because the men are great conversationalists.

A study out of Munich, Germany showed that men choose their mates based upon the relative attractiveness of the women, but that the relative attractiveness of the man has very little to do with the selection process. The study also showed that women were strikingly good at evaluating their own level of attractiveness. Basically, the more financial stability a man can offer, the more attractive his mate will be. It makes sense to me then that women are influenced by not only the earning power of their mates, but also how much of the household budgets they are allocated. On average, women do 80% of household spending and, from my observations, some rely on their mates to figure out how to earn more money if the budget is being exceeded. If the man pushes back, he risks being accused of abuse. Thus, some women seem to be wired to be *financially abusive*, which is essentially a form of extortion.

I've seen that the family court system in America favors women in this war of the sexes – the Kevin Federline exception is duly noted. If a wife is attractive enough, she can simply divorce her husband and find a new one with more money with virtually no penalty, even receiving alimony as a parting gift. On the other hand, men understand very well that trading up will cost them half of their assets plus alimony. Verbal and financial abuses are simply the result of society evolving more quickly than biology. Men still have testosterone coursing through their bodies in the same way they did 5000 years ago, and it is very difficult for them not to react with rage when half of their assets and future earnings are taken from them. When women still instinctively look for the most security they can find, conflict is inevitable.

My views on these issues come from personal experiences. For most of our marriage, Sandra resented me because I stood my ground and tried to manage our finances responsibly. I did this while she compared her station in life to that of those around her. She became irate every time I tried to keep to a budget and refused to acknowledge the consequences of her constant financial abuse. She always knew exactly what my income was, but never much cared about our savings. The Sandra I met in 1995 was very proud to tell me how independent she was and that she had trekked across Guatemala with all her belongings in a backpack. After spending a couple of years with The Foreskins, she made a point of telling me that she expected to be taken care of. It became obvious to me that her father had tried to get her to be financial responsible because on several occasions she yelled, "Don't patronize me, you're not my father!"

I thought that expecting her to live within our means was not paternalistic, but rather a reasonable expectation of my adult wife. When she overspent, she showed a complete lack of respect for my boundaries, and her accusation of abuse was nothing more than projection. If someone consistently and forcefully tells you that you are the problem, however, it becomes very difficult not to believe it.

I started to believe that there was something wrong with me, and just as I did after my conflict with my mace-wielding neighbor, I blamed myself. Since our divorce, I have reconnected with old friends and made many new friends who would offer a different view of my nature. These are the types of people that are attracted to me in spite of, or perhaps because of, the intensity of my personality.

The evolutionary benefits of anger are obvious, but how can it be useful in a happy marriage? I didn't have a good answer to that question, and I thought I loved Sandra enough to want to *fix* myself. I had often felt there was something physical causing my irritability, and even though I was most likely having physiological reactions to the constant stress of the marriage, I reached the conclusion that I needed medical intervention.

I started going to see a psychiatrist who immediately began prescribing medications to deal with the problem. I'm not a scientologist, but in my opinion, psychiatrists have become every bit as dangerous as they are portrayed to be by that group. Long gone are the days when psychiatrists were trained in psychotherapy and concentrated their efforts on the mental root causes of negative emotions. Therapy is left to psychologists while psychiatrists follow the classic Western medicine technique: diagnose as quickly as possible, then prescribe or refer. Perhaps the combination of psychologists and psychiatrists works in extreme cases, but I'm convinced that most people should avoid the medical doctors when dealing with psychological stress. In my case, the initial diagnosis involved him asking a few basic questions followed by a brief explanation of the drugs that were available to treat depression. He asked me if I wanted to try Prozac, and even though I didn't like the idea of joining Prozac Nation, I agreed to try it.

Over the next few weeks, I was occasionally very fatigued, but the intensity that I've always lived with gradually lifted. As my personality mellowed, I often felt elated, and it went through my mind that this was the way that normal people got to feel their whole lives. I was hooked. It was an illusion, and the so-called wonder drug put me in the most danger I have ever been. By the time my marriage dissolved a year and a half later, the positive benefits of the Prozac had diminished, and new effects were starting to emerge. The most perilous of these was an unpredictable surge of overwhelming hopelessness disguised as emotional reactions to my crumbling life. Any negative thought would result in an immediate, horrible sadness like one might experience when the loss of family member sinks in. It was as if I could feel the chemical reaction happening in my brain.

Emotionally, I had wanted out of my marriage, but I was neither prepared for the reality nor equipped to deal with the battle that ensued. Once Sandra had made up her mind about our future, she became very confrontational in the process of dividing the assets. She wanted to have the Curves business for herself, but I wasn't sure that was fair. Concentrating on Second Wind undistracted by another business was appealing, but I had worked hard on Curves and financed all the start-up costs. I felt like I deserved the opportunity to see how things would go once I had been in business a full year.

Sandra was insistent, however, and used my 2005 summer vacation plans to Canada to impose her will. She had her lawyer draw up a legal agreement that gave her full ownership of Curves and then waited until the day before I was to leave on the trip. She informed me she wouldn't sign the affidavit allowing the kids to leave the country with me unless I agreed to her terms. Thinking about the trip had provided me with some rare positive thoughts, so at the time, I felt I had no choice but to sign the agreement.

It was a heavy-handed use of our children as leverage, and betrayals such as this consumed me. The divorce dominated every aspect of my life, and I couldn't control the emotions I was feeling. My depression steadily intensified that fall as several things became clear: my business was not going to succeed quickly enough to support me; companies in the Raleigh area were not interested in hiring a self-employed MBA; Sandra was determined to make her new boyfriend a part of my kid's lives; and the insidious dangers of Prozac were making my situation worse.

One weekend in November 2005, I had finally had enough of life and wanted out. As I contemplated my exit, I felt myself relax, and all the things that bothered me for so many months seemed completely trivial. I quickly decided that the best way to do it would be to shoot myself in the chest. The thought of blowing out the back of my skull wasn't palatable because, in spite of everything, I still had enough arrogance left that I couldn't imagine the disfigurement of my head. My perception of America was that I could simply go to a store and pick out the weapon, so I got in my Isuzu Trooper and drove toward Durham where pawnshops abound. I was so relieved that my struggles would be ending that I felt the meaning of the words *sweet release of death.* It was an incredible, sunny day and the fall colors were at their peak. Being able to choose the circumstances of your own demise on a beautiful day is rare and, at the time, seemed right.

I often wonder how death-row inmates feel as they walk through dull, concrete block hallways toward an end that has been chosen for them. Perhaps some of them get the same sense of calm that I had, but I doubt it. I suspect that, for all but the most horrific psychopaths, the ominous and inevitable lethal injection at the end of those hallways leaves them feeling like scared little children. I once saw footage of one inmate being given a drink of water shortly before he was taken away; his hands were shaking so much that he could barely hold the cup. Maybe even pure psychopaths with the emotional capacity of animals would be overwhelmed by the fight or flight response at those moments. Their survival instinct must cause them to feel like a wolf in a leg-hold trap, only worse—they would understand what is about to happen.

I understood that it was a perfect day to die, but my plan was thwarted at the first pawnshop when I was told that I needed a permit in order to purchase a firearm. This surprised me because many Canadians are under the impression that there is no gun control in the U.S. In fact, there is; otherwise I would be dead. Of course, I had never had any previous interest in guns, so I couldn't have known. I was so impulsive in my thinking I wasn't willing to wait for a permit. Plus, it involved work. I very briefly thought of trying to get one illegally, but I had read all about the severity of gun crime punishments in America. Going to prison was not an option, so I temporarily gave up on killing myself. I had felt a calm that I knew I could easily get back at any time, so I went home and carried on with my pathetic existence.

Within a few days, I was suicidal again, but this time I wanted to say goodbye to Kyndal and Johnathan first. I called Sandra to meet me somewhere, so I could see them one last time. After an emotional visit, I left to carry out a new plan. About a year earlier when I was cutting the rubber floor for Second Wind, I had accidentally sliced my finger wide open. It was only my finger, but even with constant pressure I bled for an hour. I had heard that bleeding to death was relatively painless and that slicing down the wrists would cut arteries that don't easily clot. I could tell that Sandra had sensed something, and I wasn't taking any chances.

I checked into a hotel with alcohol and a knife and then spent most of the day drinking and watching football. Again, the idea of not having to worry about tomorrow made the day perversely enjoyable. I also wrote letters to everybody I loved, or thought I loved; although, I imagine that these writings were largely incoherent rambling.

When the letters were finished, I decided it was time and ran a bath. I got in with my carpet knife, and at first, I just sat there contemplating what it would feel like. Then, I started to think about what had brought me to this point. I'm generally an emotional person, but I've only sobbed twice in my adult life. The first time, was when I watched as one of our dogs was put to sleep. It was like watching an execution, and the emotion took me completely by surprise. As I sat there in the warm water, my sobbing was again spontaneous, but it didn't surprise me because all I could feel anymore was negative emotion. I had never before experienced another voice in my head, but now a new presence in my mind started urging me, "Do It!" I sliced down my left wrist, but I wasn't prepared for the physical pain. When I had accidentally cut myself, I almost passed out. Trying to inflict this type of damage intentionally required more mental strength than I either had or was willing to exert. Instead, I worked on creating a deep wound gradually and eventually began to bleed steadily.

After about thirty minutes in the bath, I couldn't cut anymore without excruciating pain. I knew that I hadn't done enough damage, but I was exhausted. I thought that I deserved to die painlessly, and this certainly wasn't that. I decided to get into bed with the hope that I would bleed out in my sleep. Alas, I woke up the next morning and now had a wound that would become a permanent scar. I checked out of the hotel and went back home as if nothing had happened, but when I got back to my apartment is was obvious that Sandra had been there. I deduced that she had called the authorities because a few phone numbers and the words "Involuntary Confinement" were scribbled on a pad on my desk in her writing. I wasn't too concerned because there was no proof that I had tried to harm myself, even though I was just biding my time for the next try.

The problem I did have was that the rest of the family was involved. Because Sandra had figured out what I was doing, I now had a whole mailbox full of voice messages that I needed to return. When I returned their many calls, I assured my parents that I was fine and that Sandra was exaggerating, but they absolutely didn't believe me. My parents had become aware of my drug use because Sandra told them it was the reason for our divorce. In fact, the drug use was a symptom not a cause, but that revelation combined with suicidal tendencies was enough to leave them desperate.

They frantically scrambled to do what they could from Edmonton, which involved tracking down two loyal Second Wind members, Chuck and Ed. I had become friends with them, and my mother must have begged them to intervene as they were constantly in my business for the next few days. Ed interrupted me one night while I was trying to poison myself with carbon monoxide by running my barbeque inside. He showed up unannounced and refused to leave for at least an hour. By the time he left, I actually felt marginally better and relented.

My friends couldn't watch me 24 hours a day, and nobody could yet force me to do anything I didn't want to do. I tried carbon monoxide poisoning again a few days later but awoke with nothing more than a slight headache. Unfortunately, Sandra had no choice but to honor the custody agreement she imposed upon me, and I still wanted to see my kids whenever it was my turn. One horrible night weeks after I tried to slice myself to death, the kids were staying with me at my apartment while Sandra was either out with friends or on a date. I didn't know which, but my mind was screaming. I was beyond anger thinking that I was being used as free baby-sitting while she was out having fun. I calmly spent the night with my children while I was going insane on the inside. Once I had put them to bed, I had even more time to churn.

Unable to deal with my anger, I spent the next hour drinking and searching the Internet for the best way to tie a noose. I was able to find the information I wanted and set about hanging myself. After tying the noose off and testing it out, I quickly realized that it would be a horrible death. It was too late to avoid a confrontation with police, however, because I had already left a message with Sandra telling her to come and get the kids before they woke up and discovered me.

The police were there within minutes with Sandra arriving just after them. The police came to the door with their weapons drawn presumably because they were concerned for the safety of the children. That thought never occurred to me, but when I think of it from their perspective, I can understand their concern. Far too many fathers have killed their children. Even in the most irrational moments of my life, I never for a second thought of hurting them or Sandra. (Her friends? That might have been a different story.) The cops also had to worry about whether or not I was armed. I wasn't, so they put their guns away, and asked me if they could come inside. I suppose that I didn't have to let them in, but I was not thinking clearly. Of course, once they came inside, they found the noose and had cause to take me in. Sandra swept the kids out of the apartment and into her car, but not before they saw me in the police car. With every fiber of my being, I hope that they have removed that memory from their minds forever.

I spent the next three days in involuntary commitment at Dorthea Dix hospital because of my insanity. Dix was the grayest, most depressing place I've ever been, at least in part because it was a prison not a hospital. My time there, brief as it was, seemed interminable. The entire time, I could only think about leaving, and I cannot imagine how long-term prisoners deal with their plight. By the time I got out 3 days later, my father had booked a ticket to Raleigh but had not yet arrived, so Chuck gave me a ride home. Not only was he a great friend with a good heart, but he had also had a personal history with this kind of severe depression. Forty years earlier at the age of fourteen, Chuck had been the one to find his father's body after suicide had taken him. As we drove to my apartment, I barely noticed that it was a horrible rainy day because it felt exponentially more pleasant than the dreary, windowless psychiatric hospital. I was determined never to go back there, and I had been clearly warned that I would spend progressively more time in lockup with each attempt.

My father got there within a couple of days and stayed with me for two weeks. We formulated a plan for both Second Wind and my job search, and he assured me that I would have any short-term financial support I needed. I actually became optimistic that I would either be able to make Second Wind work or find a decent job. I also realized that I had managed to make some good friends in spite of my troubles. My wife no longer had any use for me, but I at least had some redeeming value to a few.

I kept going back to one thing Chuck had said to me when he shared his story of his father with me, "I know you won't do that to your children. You're too good of a person."

His words had a tremendous impact, and I held on to the resolve they gave me for as long as I could. I also held on to the memory of staying in the cage, and I treasured my freedom enough that my depression ebbed for the next few months. I developed a routine of golfing with Chuck three times a week, running the business, seeing the kids twice a week, and dating. I also looked for jobs, but as time passed and I got no results, my efforts became more and more half-hearted. Gradually, I slid deeper than ever into depression, and in response my psychiatrist began searching for the elusive magic bullet. At various times, I had Gabapentin, Provigil, Valium, Prozac, and otherwise-obtained Hydrocodone, all actively mixed in my system. The Provigil was particularly nasty, and I could feel the strain it was putting on my body. I believe that if I hadn't been athletic my entire life, that drug could have caused heart failure.

In March 2006, I made the difficult decision to close down my business even though it had been my passion for two years, more if you consider the fact that my interest in exercise went back to childhood. At about the same time, I received news that I didn't get the only corporate job for which I was actively being considered. With Second Wind closed and no job prospects whatsoever, I now had nothing but time on my hands. Even worse, I was basically out of money. Intellectually, I knew that I could rebuild my life and put the marriage behind me, but emotionally I didn't want to.

It is difficult for me now to fully identify with the person I was at that time because it seems almost like I'm looking back at someone else, but I remember that I felt too exhausted to continue. The memory of confinement was enough to keep me from wanting to go back there, so my resolve was to be extremely careful not to botch my next attempt and get caught again. I wasn't reaching out for help anymore; I didn't want to continue. I simply wanted to be left alone to take my life in the most peaceful way I could manage. I changed the beneficiary designation of my $750,000 insurance policy because there was no way that I was going to make Sandra wealthy as a result of my demise. I also trusted my brothers more than I did her to make sure the kids were taken care of financially.

I had come to the conclusion based on my previous attempts that the best way to go would be in my sleep. I envisioned taking something that would make me drowsy, and then as I was about to pass out, I would take the lethal dosage. I did a lot of research on the Internet on various drugs, so I could know what the pain factor would be and what part of my body would be shutting down. I had most of a prescription of Valium left, but I knew that it was difficult to overdose on Valium alone. I decided to combine it with alcohol and a few Hydrocodone pills I had left. I listened to music in bed as I calmly went to sleep with no intention of waking up. I have only fleeting memories of the next 36 hours, except for trying to get up to relieve myself on several occasions. I was so weak that I had to crawl across the bedroom floor to the bathroom because I couldn't walk. I can also vaguely remember answering a phone call from one of my friends, but I can't recall what was said. Eventually, I awoke with a nasty bruise on my hip from one of my bathroom trips that caused me to limp around for days. No one ever discovered what I had done, so my freedom wasn't in jeopardy yet.

Feeling like I had actually come close to death, I spent the next couple weeks pondering what purpose there was to being on the planet and whether or not I was making the correct decision in wanting to exit it. Each time, I thought that maybe I wasn't, I considered the alternative. My thoughts weren't exactly clear-headed, but this was what I considered logical at that time—I reasoned that I was going to die eventually, so why not now? I could stick around for my children perhaps, but eventually they were going to die as will my grandchildren and so on. In time, I calculated, the universe will explode, and none of the things that happen on this planet will matter unless there is an afterlife. If there is, why not get there sooner rather than later? I certainly didn't care about the religious argument that we must toil and suffer on the planet until God decides that it is our time. The fear of going to hell for committing suicide is nothing more, I believe, than an evolutionary defense mechanism to ensure species survival. If there is no afterlife, then this entire existence we have is a cruel joke. When the universe explodes, everything that we are, were, or will be gets erased. What is the point?

My life circumstances weren't improving, and the sick calm had returned. I had been escaping into books and complete seasons of Lost and 24, but once I had finished with them, I decided that I was ready again. I was finally going to find out about what awaits us when we die, or I wouldn't, depending on what the truth is. Months earlier, when Sandra and I were fighting about my drug problem she screamed, "You like to see how close you can get to the edge, and then you pull yourself back. Sooner or later you're not going to be able to pull yourself back."

Of all the things she ever said to me, this had the most impact. It was true, but I wasn't certain why until about 3pm on April 6th, 2006. I had to get right up to the edge of oblivion and stare it down to fully grasp what she was saying. Over the course of the previous 18 hours, I had ingested alcohol, Gabapentin, and 180 Benadryl pills. I could feel my body shutting down, although it wasn't as I had expected it to be. I expected to fall asleep and not wake up, but instead the Benadryl was making me anxiously alert. As I surfed the Internet while waiting to pass out, it occurred to me that I hadn't gone to the bathroom all day, and I noticed that I was retaining water. My arms were turning red and all muscle definition was gone, so I assumed that my kidneys were beginning to shut down. I suspected that I would soon be on the carpeted floor of my apartment writhing in pain as I experienced death.

The human mind cannot fully imagine a world without it, but I sat there and tried really hard to do just that. I also tried to imagine what would come next. Would it be heaven, hell, zero, or something else? What does it feel like to be seeing your last images? The idea of complete nothingness seemed daunting, but at least it would mean that I could finally escape to peace. Then, another possibility gripped me, and it terrified me the most. The thought that I might wind up squeezing through a birth canal and starting this shit all over again sent me into a panic. I imagined myself being reincarnated into this world and having to relearn everything I had accumulated in 36 years. Even worse, I thought, I might not get to come back as a human. I contemplated the existence of a feral beast, and my current plight seemed far less dismal. No wonder that as newborns we fall so unconditionally in love with those who are there to guide us into this incredibly frightening place.

It took a near self-inflicted death for me to realize that I wanted to hold onto that consciousness for as long as I could. I had to get right up to that edge to see the payoff of all my efforts.

I got up and walked around my apartment trying to figure out what to do. What happened next is a blur of activities that I remember this way. I thought I heard a faint chatter as if a group of people were just around the corner conversing in hushed tones. That unnerved me even more, so I called 911 and told them that I had taken too many pills. The operator immediately called for an ambulance and then insisted that I stay on the line until it arrived. It was obvious that her job was to keep me talking. She prodded me for more information about what I had taken, how much, and why.

Before long, I could hear the siren of the ambulance, but it didn't seem to be getting any closer. The apartment complex I lived in was large and hard to navigate, so I figured out that they were lost. I put the phone down with the 911 operator's voice still trailing through it and walked down to the parking lot so that I could flag the paramedics down when they drove past in the ambulance. Eventually, they either saw me or figured out where I was.

I began answering the same questions for the paramedics that I had answered for the 911-operator. Unlike the operator, however, one of the paramedics clearly seemed irritated with me. In a very accusatory way, he questioned me about the scar on my wrist that I had covered with a Band-Aid. Under other circumstances, I might have been irritated back, but then I just wanted to get into the ambulance because my vision was starting to change. It wasn't just blurry but definitely distorted, as if I were looking through water. It was distracting enough that I didn't pay much attention to the small crowd that had gathered or the police car that had arrived. After several questions, they helped me into the ambulance and took me to the emergency room.

On the way to the hospital, the conversation was far less adversarial. One of the paramedics and I talked about the reasons that I had taken the overdose. I'm guessing that I'm not the first suicidal person he had dealt with because he seemed to know how to make me feel better. For the most part, we talked about the kids and how much they meant to me. I told him that I was having trouble finding a job and that was a major factor in my depression. He made the suggestion that maybe I would have to move away from Raleigh, which I immediately dismissed.

"My children are here. I can't leave them," I countered.

"Don't you think that your children are better off with you alive somewhere else than close by and miserable or dead?" And that was it; his words formed the basis for my decisions over the next two years. In this brutal, unfair world we live in, I knew he was right.

At the hospital, I was immediately taken to an ICU room where I was hooked up to a heart monitor and IV. As they were doing this, the doctor was asking me the same questions that the 911-operator and paramedics had.

"What did you take?" he asked

"Mostly Benadryl," I told him as I had the others.

"How many?"

"About 180," I whispered. My voice was almost gone because of the dryness I was feeling in my throat.

"180," he repeated incredulously. "Are you sure?"

"Yes,"

"How are you still alive?"

The question was rhetorical, but it is something I still wonder about to this day. Nobody knows for sure how quickly time passes in a dying mind, and given my disoriented condition, I wondered if I had actually passed out before I called 9-1-1. It seemed very possible to me that these were just the last thoughts I conjured up before everything went black and that I was really still lying on the floor of my apartment. I spent the next few hours in a state of semi-consciousness and have only vague recollections. At least once that I can remember, the nurse came rushing in because my blood pressure dropped and my heart started racing. In a few hours, however, they got me fully stabilized.

I stayed under close watch, but they mostly left me alone to recover. With nothing to drown it out, the whispering returned, and I was certain that I could hear my family in the next room. Their conversation about doing an intervention as soon as I got out seemed completely real to me, but I could no longer separate my imagination from reality.

On the positive side, my normal body functions returned as evidenced by my constant trips to the restroom. Unfortunately, I had to have company every time I went to the bathroom. The doctor had recommended that I be committed again, a judge had signed the order while I was recovering, and I was now officially in police custody for the second time in my life. When I was released, the cop put me in handcuffs and led me out of the hospital to be taken to another hospital. I expected to see my family as I left the hospital but they were not around. I was taken by ambulance to Holly Hills, an up-market version of Dorthea Dix, and turned over to the custody of a female administrator. She frisked me and took me into the secure area of the facility, where I would remain for the next seven days.

As I walked into the main foyer, it was busy with activity. There seemed to be about twenty people going about their pre-bedtime business, but only one person in the room caught my attention. A man with long, scraggly blond hair, which flowed behind him as he walked across the room, had eyes that completely mesmerized me. They were a brilliant blue that I had never seen before, and when contrasted against the grayness of his face, they pierced right into me. He seemed to be sizing me up, and my mind immediately went back to thinking that I was dying.

In my disorientation, I believed that this crazy looking person was actually an angel, and I was in some sort of a purgatory. I was then taken to my room, only to find out that this person was my roommate. Because of this, and the fact that my family had seemingly disappeared, I had a mild panic attack. I was able to calm myself, but up until the time I was released, I had the overwhelming need to get back to my apartment to verify that my body wasn't lying in the middle of the living room.

I have never fully recovered from the damage of that overdose. Occasionally, I still get a deja-vu sense of things, and it takes me back to wondering if I never actually made that 9-1-1 call. Logically, I know that this is not a dream, but there will always be that sliver of doubt. Whenever the fear grips me, I just remind myself that I've experienced a very full existence since then, so if this is what is happening, our last moments are not so bad.

I was still in a state of confusion the next day when I called my brother, Owen, from the phone in the common area. I couldn't understand why they hadn't come to see me during visiting hours when I could hear them talking in the lobby. All I had was the jean shorts and a t-shirt I was wearing when I left my apartment, and I was irritated that they hadn't at least thought to bring me a change of clothes.

"Owen."

"Warren." My family still calls me by first name.

"Where are you? I need some clothes," I said this as if he should have known everything that was going on.

"What do you mean?"

"I'm in the hospital. You know that."

"What are you talking about?" he asked, and a wave of dread gripped me. I finally realized that I had imagined everything about my family being in the next room. What else had I imagined? *Sherwood!* I had left him in my apartment, and he had been on his own for at least 24 hours. I quickly explained to Owen what had happened, hung up, and immediately called the only person I could think of to save my dog.

I called Sandra because I was too distraught to be proud, and he had been her dog too. Through it all, Sherwood was there, and I was terrified that he could have been left alone to die. I explained to her that I was in the hospital and that she had to go get him. By the time she got there, he had been in the house by himself for almost two days, but he was fine and had even waited to go to the bathroom. He is a very special friend.

It took another two days before I was completely free of hallucinations, and by that time, my parents had arrived in Raleigh. Sandra and Owen had obviously made the rest of the family aware of what I had done, and my parents had come to deal with the situation. I was allowed to see them in a private room, and I sat down at a table across from them.

"How did you get here son?" was the first thing my father asked.

"I don't know," I said because I knew he wasn't asking about the ambulance ride from my apartment. He wanted to know how his oldest child could have reached such a point in his life, and I couldn't explain it. My mother was a wreck and could barely function at that point, but my father was the strength the entire family needed. He possesses a steely resolve that he inherited from his mother. My Grams marched through life doing what she needed to do regardless of the situation. My father did everything that needed to be done, and in every way, I would not be alive today but for him. When I was released from the hospital, he took me back to Canada and for weeks provided the stability that both my mother and I needed to get through the crisis. I strive to someday have that same type of strength for my children.

Having stared down all the possibilities of our next phase, what happens after death, I'm at peace with all of them, but my experience often makes me think about the death penalty debate. If people commit crimes so heinous that they are no longer welcome in society, what should we do with them? The crux of the matter is which punishment is worse, confinement or oblivion? I would prefer to be put down than rotting in a cell thinking about my crimes, but I have a conscience. Psychopaths, who apparently do not possess a conscience, have no such problem and probably prefer self-preservation. So should we kill them? It is a question that juries have to answer every day.

CHAPTER 14 – SITUATIONAL INSANITY

For several moments, I stand completely still letting the water run down over the back of my head and then onto the rest of my body. Nobody is waiting, and I am in no hurry to abandon the warmth. The dressing rooms are cold and dirty enough that I usually shower at home, but I am in the mood to extend the rare feeling of victory at the rink. My new team is bad, and the season is quickly becoming a write-off. That's frustrating, but I'm not going to change teams again after having quit the White team nine months earlier. Besides, an impressive 10-0 win has given me reason for optimism, and I really didn't know how long I am going to stay in Los Angeles anyway.

I have recovered well enough that I'm giving serious consideration to moving back to North Carolina. Sandra's antics no longer bother me beyond how they affect our kids, and looking for a job when I already have a decent one is not stressful. Unfortunately, I am still having no success, largely because of the closed-off nature of the Raleigh job market. On several occasions, I have recruiters say things like, "If you're ever out here, give me a call."

Fortunately, I have been off Prozac and other such psychotropic drugs for over a year, and my obstinate personality is fully restored. As far as I am concerned, the Southern hicks with their provincial attitudes are free to go fuck themselves. Nobody is going to stop me from getting a good job there, and I am determined to again be a part of my children's day-to-day lives. In spite of my resolve, it is now November, and I've spent the majority of 2007 working on trying to get that perfect job that will enable me to return to my kids.

I'm contemplating all this and looking down at the plastic mat on the tiled shower floor when I hear the door to the dressing room open.

"I'm looking for Mike Korkie," a male voice says to the two other players who remain.

Through the shower opening to my right, I can see one of my teammates pointing me out to a relatively fit, middle-aged man I don't recognize.

"I want to meet you when you're done," he says, as we make eye contact.

"OK," I say, and with that, he backs out of the room letting the door close behind him.

"Who was that?" I am immediately asked.

I have no idea and just shrug, but I know it can be about only one thing. The real question is how the hell they found me here. I'm not even playing at Culver City anymore, and I haven't told anyone associated with Graeme where I'm playing. Granted there aren't that many rinks in L.A., but this one is at least an hour from Culver. The police have my phone number if they want more information, so I have no idea what this guy could want. By the time I'm sitting down on the bench putting my socks on, he has returned. I am slightly apprehensive, but as he stands in front of me, I quickly realized I have nothing to worry about.

He is very cordial, and, as we shake hands, he smiles pleasantly, "I'm Riley Sherman, Graeme's lawyer."

This, I was definitely not expecting. In my mind, I was completely invisible to the non-hockey world late on a Monday evening in the middle of the San Fernando Valley.

My facial expression must have betrayed my amazement, so he continues, "I play on the Wolves. I saw your name on the scoring leaders list, and I just want to meet you."

I had underestimated just how small the hockey community is, even in a city of 16 million. Of course Graeme's lawyer is a hockey player, and of course we play in the same league.

"Nice to meet you," I say as he sits down next to me on the bench. "How's he doing?"

"Well, he's in jail," he says. It is an obvious statement, and the implied meaning is clear: not good.

"I'm surprised that you came to see me. I left you a message a few weeks ago, but I never heard back from you."

Apparently, he has no recollection of getting a message from me, or it just wasn't given to him. Graeme's former assistant, Lindsay, had asked me to call his lawyers, and I did, expecting a professional reply. I never got one, and even as we speak face-to-face, he seems to be avoiding the issue of the criminal proceedings. When I finally ask direct questions about it, he tells me that he hasn't come to talk about the case. I could understand that there are probably a lot of things that he isn't allowed to talk about, but then why come to see me at all? I can only surmise that he is curious about the mystery roommate who knows everything about the events that led up to Graeme's incarceration. He may want to size me up to see what he will be dealing with if I am called to testify.

We sit there and chat mostly about hockey, but I continue to subtly prod him for details of the case. Eventually, he opens up slightly and asks a rhetorical question, "How can someone who's been a committed family man for thirty years do something like this?" He continues, "There's a case for situational insanity when it comes to that woman, and I'm the one who has to defend him."

The rest of the conversation is pleasant but not very enlightening, and he soon leaves for his game. Part of me wants to be polite and send Graeme my best through his lawyer, but it wouldn't have been sincere. I am completely disgusted with him and haven't spoken to him since the end of February. After everything that has happened, Graeme is still in contact with Jasmine proving that he has, in fact, gone completely insane.

Back in early January, Lindsay conceded that Graeme had ruined his business beyond repair when she quit and moved to Texas. Perhaps if Graeme's drug use hadn't been so out of control, she might have stayed while the paychecks kept coming. As it was, however, he had asked her to commit a felony by holding on to his drug stash and keeping track of how much he was using. Meting out his cocaine would have been an absolute no-win situation for her, and she really had no choice but to move on.

I had previously predicted that Lindsay's departure would be one of the signs of Graeme's final death spiral, and in a way, I got to witness that plummet, almost like watching a child run into traffic from inside a house.

* * *

The marketing department for Universal Studios Hollywood does promotions with the L.A. Kings, and the deals include the use of an event suite. I was given a pair of tickets and considered taking Graeme, but initially I decided not to. I was concerned that he could damage my reputation at work if anyone noticed the ever-present white shmeg around the corners of his nose. I was also worried about his reaction if he found out about the Amgen job lie. I had told him a month earlier that my contract at Amgen had ended, but if he spent too much time talking to my coworkers, he might have figured out that I had been working in Universal City all along. After due consideration, I decided that it was worth the risk taking him with me to the event suite as a way of thanking him for looking after Sherwood at Christmas.

At first, he turned me down, so I was somewhat relieved when I hung up the phone. I had made a nice offer, but he wasn't interested. Fine with me. Within thirty seconds, though, he rang back.

"What was I thinking? Of course I'll take a free ticket to watch a game in a luxury suite."

He had become so conditioned to picking up the tab for Jasmine that his first instinct in response to a request was to say no, thereby saving himself a few bucks. Once he realized that someone was actually doing something nice for him, he jumped at the opportunity.

I made arrangements to meet him outside of the rink, so that if he looked like a complete wreck, I could figure out a way to abort the whole thing. When I saw him, there were no obvious signs of drug use, so I took him inside. By the time we got to the suite, most of the group was already there and involved in private conversations, which was ideal. Other than some obligatory small talk, Graeme and I were left alone to watch the game at our own table. With the crowd noise and the commotion of twenty people watching a hockey game, I felt comfortable talking about the latest salacious details of his life.

When he told me about Lindsay quitting, he was visibly upset, but in typical Graeme fashion, he deluded himself into thinking that his new situation was even better. He had replaced Lindsay with the Gooch, who was going to be more than just a personal assistant. He also held the titles of personal trainer and bodyguard.

"Why do you need a bodyguard?" I asked.

"You know, just in case," he replied.

In saying this, he was acknowledging the danger of his lifestyle, but he was also stating loud and clear that he wasn't willing to change a thing. Most people, when confronted with the realization that they need a bodyguard, might be prompted to change their habits. Not Graeme. Like so many other things in his life, having a bodyguard gave him a false sense of importance. Gooch was also living with Graeme, so the duties were 24-7; although, I doubted that there was any real work being done. I was obviously in no position to judge, having flopped in that house myself a few short months earlier.

Later on, Graeme asked me, "Are you still seeing Jody?" I could tell by his manner that the topic wasn't spontaneous; he had been planning to bring it up.

"No," I replied firmly.

"Can you get in touch with her?"

"No, I don't have her number. I told you before when it's over with a woman I delete her number from my cell phone," I said. Rather than tell him for the 50th time that he should do the same thing with Jasmine's number, I asked, "Why?"

"I want to talk to her."

"What for?" I pressed.

He squirmed a little bit on his stool, "Jasmine and I were talking about it, and we want to try and turn her out."

"What do you mean?" I was pretty sure I knew what he was trying to say, but I wanted him to clarify.

"We think that we can get her turning tricks and take a cut for ourselves."

"Are you out of your mind?"

"No. She's desperate; Jasmine thinks we could do it."

"She's not that desperate, Graeme." I was amazed at what he was suggesting, and I was insulted for both Jody and myself. If nothing else, she was not to be trifled with and probably would have stabbed a fork in Graeme's eye just for suggesting it. Plus, I knew for a fact that she owned a gun, so trying to force her into prostitution would have been a dangerous endeavor. I wanted to punch him for insinuating that a hot chick that slept with me could only be a hooker. The crack whore probably initiated that line of thinking, so I put those feelings aside and continued, "Well I don't have her number and even if I did, I guarantee you, she wouldn't do it."

"Hmmp," was the only reaction he could muster, and I could tell that he was frustrated. Not being able to get Jody's number was interfering with Graeme and Jasmine's coke-fueled fantasy. Judging by the look on his face, the plan wasn't dead. As soon as they could figure out how to find her, he and Jasmine were gonna be pimps.

This conversation was the final tipping point on my opinion of Graeme's true character. He had previously admitted things that hinted at a lack of morality but nothing more serious than fraud and relatively minor deceptions. In case he ever got stopped for a DUI check, he practiced the alphabet backwards and had researched a list of medications that could make your breath smell like alcohol. When the Northridge earthquake damaged his home, he had taken a sledgehammer to the walls to ensure that he would get a settlement. Before Jasmine, I had thought that most of this type of behavior indicated mental weakness rather than danger. Now, he was willing to destroy the life of someone I knew in order to feed his drug habit. She was nothing more than an object for him to utilize. It was a clear symptom of how close he was to complete meltdown, and I knew that I could no longer trust him. I didn't take the insult personally, however, because he had become a narcissistic addict flailing away for drug money. I realized that nothing he might do to fund his habit should be surprising.

Cast in this new light, the financial dealings of his wife Julia's estate and his bankruptcy now seemed much more sinister. Sarah had told me that Julia died of an accidental drug overdose because that is the story that came from Graeme. Apparently, Ryan had discussed the toxicology report with the coroner and the results were inconclusive. He constantly argued with his father about the money, and I suspected that there was probably another fraud being perpetrated. During one discussion of the lawsuit, Graeme expressed a simplification of the biggest problem he had, "if it walks like a duck and talks like a duck..." I inferred then that he was, in fact, in control of the assets, and he needed to protect that secret. The circumstances of Julia's death were incredibly suspicious when one considers how much

Graeme had to gain from her being dead. She was a known drug abuser and an easy target for someone with a criminal mind. I wondered if the emotion he showed while going through Julia's closet was merely an act.

After the game, we went our separate ways, and I kept my distance from him until he showed up unexpectedly in Culver City for one of our league games. I guessed that it had been at least two months since he had played, so I thought it was going to be an unmitigated disaster. In the dressing room before the game, he had a dreamy look on his face, and his eyes were bulging. To my great surprise, he wound up having one of the better games that I had ever seen him play, and I knew that he must have snorted a mountain to get up for that game. I cringed at the stress it would have put on his heart.

When I called him later that week to see if he was coming to our next league game, I used the opportunity to try to get him to explain why he was so gripped by the cocaine high. He was risking death, and even self-destructive people have to get some benefit from their poison.

"What's the attraction?" I asked him.

"It gets me going. Sometimes, I just do a half a line if I have a lot of work to do. It's like a really strong cup coffee," he explained.

"Then why not just have some coffee?" I challenged. Coffee I do understand.

"You're right, but you're not right," he replied. Translation: you are absolutely 100% correct, but I refuse to listen to your logic. I pressed him a little more to see if he, at some level, had a better understanding of his own situation, but he was evasive and illogical for the rest of the conversation. There was no way that anything I could say was going to change his mind.

Graeme's inadequate argument did very little to change my mind, based upon my own experience, that cocaine is a useless drug. I had encountered more users in my first few months in L.A. than I had my entire life, so drugs were obviously readily available. Back in university, magic mushrooms had fueled one of the best parties I had ever attended, so for several months, I asked my new friends about getting some. Ironically, the only recreational drug that I was interested in seemed to be the only one that was unattainable in my network.

James was one of the people I had asked on several occasions, so one night as he had several times before, he suggested 'candy' instead. This was prior to Graeme's collapse, but even then, the idea of putting powder up my nose was not appealing. It always reminded me of sophomoric practical jokes played with pepper. I tried it anyway, and it did absolutely nothing for me except make my heart skip the odd beat or two.

In hindsight, I'm very lucky that my brain chemistry is not turned on by cocaine. The drug that destroyed Graeme had no effect on me; whereas, opiates were a major contributor to my own involuntary confinement. Ultimately, this type of randomness in effect is the scariest part of severe addiction and the mental illness that accompanies it. People can be intolerant of others with these issues, something I've experienced first-hand.

When I was in the emergency room recovering from my overdose, I heard the cop ask the doctor, "Is he going to be all right?"

"Physically, he'll be fine. He just needs to get the cartilage removed from his brain," the doctor replied.

That's some old-school thinking right there. The fact that psychiatrists view themselves as doctors treating patients with a legitimate disease contrasts directly with how the mentally ill are actually treated by so-called caregivers in emergency rooms. My experience as a patient in that E.R. was that they seemed to feel that I was bringing the problems on myself, and they had no patience for me. The cops I dealt with acted far more compassionately than the health care workers. Most likely this was because most of the people they deal with pose some sort of a threat to them; I was only a threat to myself.

When I now reflect on the doctor's comment, I am struck by how little things have changed in the 15 years since I worked as a porter in the University of Alberta hospital E.R. On many occasions, we had mentally ill people come in, and I vividly remember hospital personnel having the attitude that they were wasting valuable resources. If you asked each of these professionals how they view mental illness, they would answer that it is a disease and people afflicted by it need care. That may be how they think of it, intellectually, but I routinely witnessed nurses shouting at patients out of frustration. I saw them roll their eyes with disdain at the people who were acting strangely.

If I had gone in with a ruptured appendix, hospital personnel would have been extremely compassionate, but given my circumstances, they weren't. I don't fault them because, deep in our psyche, we don't want to deal with the mentally ill; evolution has required this. If a caveman broke his leg, two of his buddies could grab him and drag him away from the lion that was trying to eat them. If something went wrong with a caveman's mental wiring, however, he had to be abandoned. When the lion was charging, they didn't have time to argue with the guy running toward it let alone try understand why he was doing it. The things we don't understand are most frightening, so by having disdain for the mentally ill, we can distance ourselves and feel secure that it will never happen to us.

Graeme was rushing straight toward the lion, which was perhaps why his plight was a regular topic of conversation in the hockey community. I had as much information as anyone, so I was asked about him constantly. Everyone was fascinated by how he went from being a fixture around the rink to being completely absent. Each week we bantered about whether or not he was going to make a surprise appearance, but by early February, he had played his last hockey game.

Graeme had helped me "remove the cartilage from my brain" as the doctor had suggested, so I didn't like the morbid curiosity about his circumstances, which, I have to admit, I had my part in. To compensate for this, I was determined not to completely abandon him. James and I decided to go out with him the first weekend in February to see just how bad the situation had gotten. We also reasoned that any night he was with us was better than the alternative. As usual, he wanted to go to Aqua because he had, of course, become great friends with the owner and all the bouncers. This would make it easy to get in, and since it was in Beverly Hills we knew it was relatively safe.

We arranged to meet at Graeme's place first, and when I got there, I had to walk past Grant's formerly beautiful car in the driveway. The black BMW now had major dents and scrapes running the length of both sides of the car. More striking was that I could tell that the damage had been in at least two different accidents. Months earlier I had noticed some minor panel damage on one side of his brand new car, which was now significantly worse. I was going to ask about it as soon as I went inside, but Graeme didn't come out of his master suite for several minutes. When he finally appeared, he was wearing jeans but was shirtless. It was obvious that he had wanted to show off his body because, after a quick hello, he started talking about how great he looked.

While he had lost a tremendous amount of weight, it did not look healthy. I estimated that at least fifteen of the pounds he had lost were muscle mass, and his physique had become very much like Grant's, except without all the tattoos.

"Now that I've lost all this weight, Gooch is going to train me up in the gym, and I'll be in great shape," he declared.

"That'll be hard on your heart with all the coke you're doing," I said.

"No, I've been checked out by my doctor. My heart is fine," he countered.

"You told him you're doing coke?" I asked with moderate surprise.

"Yep, he says my heart is just fine. He says I'm an idiot, but my heart is fine."

I could imagine how that conversation really went, but in Graeme's mind he had been given a clean bill of health to snort away.

There was nothing he couldn't distort to fit his view of the world. Some minutes later, still on the topic of his health, he admitted, "I have a manic disorder. I'm not bipolar, but I do have a type of manic disorder."

I'm not sure how he distinguished manic disorder from bipolar disorder, but something about that subtle distinction made him feel better. I think it allowed him to reverse the cause-effect of his drug use and erratic behavior. Cocaine is very popular amongst manic-depressives, but I had never seen him in any erratic cycles while I was living with him. He didn't want the stigma of bipolar, but if he could make himself believe that he had a disorder and that disorder caused him to use drugs, then any problems that resulted weren't really his fault. Most importantly, he gave himself a clear conscience to continue his drug abuse.

I didn't feel like helping him justify, so I changed the subject, "What happened to Grant's car?"

Graeme just shook his head sadly and for a brief moment in time became an exasperated father who wished his son would get his act together. Grant's predicament was almost as bad as his father's: he was recklessly driving around without a license and the cops were looking for him for assaulting a woman, presumably another relationship that ended badly.

"He has to be using more than just weed," I told him referring to our previous conversation about Grant's drug abuse.

"He's been using ecstasy. We call it E." The "we" he was referring to was the hip, hard-core drug using community, in which he now proudly included himself. I could tell that he loved defining himself this way, but the drug subculture is nothing more than a pyramid scheme. It's an economy that operates almost completely independently of the rest of society, except there is no real work being done. Nobody involved with that type of hard living can maintain a job, but there is room for some participants to stake out a position at the top of the pyramid by dealing in drugs or prostitution. The rest of the pyramid, however, has to be supported by outside resources. Those at the bottom bring in their money and often lose everything in the process.

Graeme was at the bottom, and his new friends had no use for him beyond his money. He needed to sell Jody into prostitution and move up the hierarchy before everything he had was gone. Most fathers don't want their kids to destroy their lives with drugs, but Graeme had even more reason for wanting his kids clean. If Grant spent all his money on drugs and car accidents, he would have no money to give to his father.

"I thought you asked his dealer not to sell him anything like that." I couldn't resist saying I told you so.

He ignored the comment and continued, "He's been taking it every day for four months. It's not meant to be taken every day."

Neither is cocaine, I thought.

By the time James showed up, Graeme had his shirt on and had shifted again from concerned father back to party animal. We made our way to Aqua where we were ushered right past the long line and into the club. Like the other times I had been there, the crowd was mostly black, and this time they were actually shooting a rap video. The bass was churning, moving the crowd, and we could see some of the activity in the VIP room. The rappers were up on a small stage holding fists full of money while posing with beautiful, dancing blonds. The atmosphere energized Graeme, and he became noticeably animated. His shoulders bobbed up and down as he scanned the main room.

"It's time for me to go to work," he said as I got my first drink.

"What do you mean?" I asked.

"This is my job. This is how I work now," inadvertently admitting that he no longer had any income. I scoffed to myself about his new job but made no comment because I recalled the business plan he had asked me to write after my last visit to

Aqua. Even though I knew he would never follow through, I had no interest in saying something that might lead to another work commitment.

My silence seemed to compel him to add more, "There's also a good chance that I'm going to get the Tyson case."

"How are you going to get that?" I asked. I didn't try to hide the cynicism in my voice.

"One of my friends has a contact," he said as if Tyson was his best friend.

"I thought that you don't do criminal law," I challenged.

"I don't, but I'm going to oversee it. With a case this big you need someone to manage all the lawyers involved." That may have been a true statement, but there was absolutely no way Mike Tyson would ever hire Graeme Bercham, although the irony of such a thing would have been amazing. Tyson had been busted for cocaine possession and was facing more prison time for violating his parole. Mike Tyson wouldn't be stupid enough to hire a fellow cokehead to represent him, but Graeme was certain that he had struck gold.

More and more, Graeme was desperately trying to cash in on boatloads of easy money, and with all his new connections, he honestly believed that he would soon be fantastically rich.

"I'm putting together all these deals, and as soon as one of them hits, it's going to be huge. I'm looking for people to run the businesses because I don't want to do that. I'll just make the contacts and put the right people together," he said.

I had encountered this type of wishful thinking my entire adult life, and it always irritated me. Everybody wants to be an overnight sensation. Even when I was in business school, almost everyone there talked about starting their own business, but they all wanted to do it without quitting their comfortable day jobs. It doesn't work that way, and when it comes down to make or break, 99% of the big-talkers aren't willing to do what is necessary. What Graeme wanted was the same thing every other faux entrepreneur wants: someone else to take on all the risk, put in all the effort, but then share the profits. Kind of like being a pimp.

"When I get rich, I'm going to give most of the money away. I don't need a lot, just enough to be comfortable. I'm going to share most of it with young people." Before Jasmine, Graeme spoke of his friends that I hadn't met, and when he did, I had always pictured whites. By this time, I had learned to see blacks, and I imagined the posse of young black friends he dreamed of bringing along on his fantastic journey. He had to do something soon though. If he didn't come up with some money, they wouldn't be his friends for much longer.

Talking about his grand scheme was enough to motivate him to get into the crowd and network. For the next thirty minutes, I observed Graeme in his element. He joked with strangers and struck up several conversations. Each time he would listen with rapt attention to whatever was being said, as if each person in there might hold his ticket to riches. He had taken to carrying around reading glasses and sticking one of the arms in his mouth as he listened, almost like he was holding a pipe. It added to the effect and perhaps deflected attention away from the corners of his nose.

He flitted about the room until finally, in his exuberance, he tried to go into the kitchen area to network with whoever happened to be in there. Very quickly, he was mildly reprimanded and politely guided back into the bar area. He tried to cover his embarrassment by having a five-minute conversation with the doorman involved, but when he came back over to where I was standing he was more subdued. I preferred this because he was now in the mood to discuss reality. Even though Graeme and Jasmine were not even close to being a couple, she still dominated his life.

"You should have seen Jasmine the other night. She got all dolled up and walked in here. The whole place stopped. I mean, she looked like a million bucks," he said with awe in his voice.

I highly doubted that anybody but Graeme really took much notice of Jasmine because she had a hold on him like I have never seen. She certainly got the reaction that she would have wanted from him, but I doubt that he was her target that night. She must have had a chip on her shoulder about something, and she was out to break hearts or crack skulls.

"She and Gooch really got into it that night. We had to pull them apart to keep them from killing each other."

Further evidence that things in Graeme's life were getting more and more turbulent, but he thrived on the drama that she created.

"I had a gun pulled on me that night," he said matter-of-factly.

"By who?"

"One of my friends."

I didn't know what to say other than ask, "Why do you let those people in your home?"

"They're nice people, but the situation got carried away. They gained a lot of respect for me though."

"Why do you think that?"

"Because of the way I handled it. I stayed calm and showed a lot of class. I think they really respected that," he told himself, as he looked me straight in the eyes. They had absolutely no respect for him, and this story just proved it.

At about 11:30, while the rappers were in the middle of a song on the main stage, the Fire Marshall shut the place down. By the standards of any other city in North America, it was a normal Saturday night sized crowd, but in Beverly Hills, the party was now over. I had seen enough and was ready to go home anyway, but Graeme was determined to keep the evening going. He begged us to come over to his place for an after-party. I had to go back to pick up my car, so James and I went to the house while Graeme and Gooch set about looking for prospective partiers. When we got to Graeme's house, we waited for 45 minutes before I finally called him to see where he was.

"Hello," he answered.

"Hey, what's going on, Graeme? I'm gonna head home," I told him.

"No, don't go anywhere. We're working on it."

I had made up my mind to leave, but decided to have some fun with him first, "You know when we go to your house there were two big black guys casing it."

First there was five seconds of dead silence before he finally said, "What!? What did they look like?"

We had known each other for long enough that I was surprised that he didn't see right through me, "No, I'm just kidding; there was nobody here."

"Don't even joke about that. We've been having some trouble with that lately," he said in a deadly serious tone. Wow! Had I, quite literally, hit close to home, and I should have known that people would be stealing from him. Not only had he opened his home to a bunch of losers, but he also had expensive possessions and mounds of cocaine. Of course people were casing his house on a regular basis – I was getting the hell out of there.

I hung up with Graeme and told James to have fun, but that was probably not the best advice given James' propensity for getting into trouble. When I called him the next day and found out how the rest of the night went, I was very glad about my decision to leave. Graeme eventually showed up without Gooch because they had gotten into some sort of disagreement. He also hadn't been able to find anyone to come back to the house for the party, so James called out for a hooker. The two of them stayed up all night doing lines and then trying to maintain a hard-on long enough to fuck. According to James, Graeme would disappear into the bathroom for half-hour at a time.

"Dude, that shit he's doing is crazy. It's too powerful," James told me.

"Really?" I asked, but I wasn't surprised because Graeme had bragged that he got the best stuff in L.A. I had known James to do a lot of cocaine, so he would know if Graeme's drugs were dangerously potent.

He continued, "It's so strong it's fucking up his tongue."

"What do you mean?" I had never heard of such a thing.

"He showed me the hole he's got in the back of his tongue. You could fit the end of a Q-tip in it; it's disgusting."

I really couldn't get a mental picture of the lesion on his tongue, but I deduced that his sinus cavity was effectively destroyed. More troubling, James told me that he overheard Graeme asking some woman at the bar about crack, and he was taking a great interest in what she had to say. Crack is much more cost-effective, and given his financial problems, it was now inevitable that he would start smoking his cocaine.

I changed the subject slightly, "Did he tell you that someone pulled a gun on him? And he thinks that they gained respect for him because of the way he handled it."

"They're laughing at him. He thinks they think he's some cool old guy, but they're really just laughing at him." I had to agree 100 percent.

* * *

Two weeks later, I had another trip to North Carolina, and Graeme was still nice enough to look after Sherwood. When I went over to drop him off on my way to the airport, Graeme was home. It was early evening, so I figured that things would be relatively tame inside and went in to thank him. We visited in the dining room, where Graeme informed me that Gooch was no longer living there. His continued altercations with Jasmine had led Graeme to kick him out, most likely for everybody's safety. Ironically, he had moved into the very same townhouse that I was supposed to be renting, although probably not paying rent.

When I looked through the living room into the den, I could see a young black couple sitting on the couch. We made eye contact and exchanged greetings.

"Who are they?" I asked quietly.

He told me their names, which I promptly forgot, and then added, "They're a really nice couple."

They were pleasant looking people, but they were also obviously high. They had that peaceful facial expression that the cocaine high brings.

"We're creating a philosophy club," he added.

"What's that?" I asked even though the name was descriptive enough. I guessed that he had gotten the idea from Ryan's school, and this was another way for him to act like a twenty-year-old.

"It's just a group of people who get together and discuss interesting topics. You should come; it's going to be really fun."

The last thing I wanted to do was listen to his dangerous friends talking stupidly about inane topics. Before I could give him a pat answer like, "yeah maybe", I noticed something that immediately changed the topic. A red trickle of blood diluted by mucus and cocaine spontaneously ran out of his left nostril past the side of his mouth and got to his jaw line before I told him, "Graeme, your nose is bleeding,"

I was taken aback because if I hadn't told him, he wouldn't have noticed, and he hadn't appeared high. Stoned was now his normal. He quickly wiped the blood away and was embarrassed for the rest of our conversation, which I kept mercifully short. I continued on my trek to the airport and then on to Raleigh, where I spent the Presidents Day weekend with the kids. It was, as always, an expensive trip worth every penny, but the financial burden was eased because I didn't have to board Sherwood. Graeme Bercham is easily the most flawed person I have ever known, but to this day, I appreciate his generosity.

With the long weekend, late night flights and work, it was four or five days before I was ready to pick Sherwood up. During this time and a few days before, I had been letting my beard grow out enough to shave into a Vandyke, so when I drove onto his street, my appearance had changed slightly. I parked across from his house and could see that he was standing in his driveway. I got out and walked over to him, but as I did, he glared at me without saying anything, while reaching his hand into his favorite tan sport coat.

When I got within twenty feet of him, I said, "Hey Graeme. What's up?"

Immediately, recognition replaced the confusion that had shown on his face. He took his hand out of his jacket, and said flatly, "Oh, it's you. I didn't recognize you with your facial hair; you should let people know when you do that."

Unlike my last visit, this time I could tell that he was stoned out of his mind. He was showing signs of extreme paranoia; his eyes were not focusing well, and his hair was unkempt. It was dark outside, but had he been sober he would have recognized me before I even got out of my car.

I had no response other than to say, "I guess. Thanks again for looking after Sherwood." Sherwood had heard my voice or recognized the sound of my car and was waiting at the gate for me. We let him out, and the three of us began walking toward my car. As we did, a brand new, white Mercedes pulled up and stopped in front of the house about forty feet from where we standing. I could see Grant inside the car, but he didn't get out. He looked like a man possessed, one who wanted to crawl out of his skin. He knew that I was there but refused to make eye contact with me as he waited for me to leave. The change in his demeanor was very concerning because he had been friendly every other time I had encountered him. This time he looked like he was ready to lash out at anyone in his vicinity.

"He got a new car," I commented, "How's he doing? He looks terrible."

Graeme filled me in on the current state of their relationship, which was not good. Grant had a mysterious benefactor, a man somehow associated with his mother, who had given him in excess of $100,000. For some reason, Grant was going to give it back, but Graeme was trying to convince him to keep it, obviously so he could get his hands on some of it. Grant's behavior had gotten so erratic and violent that he had swung a baseball bat at Graeme. He gave no indication of what had caused the fight, but drugs and money most certainly factored in. Graeme also told me that he had taken to sleeping with a gun, and while he didn't come right out and say it, I was sure that he was also carrying it around with him. As our conversation continued, I could tell that Grant was getting more and more agitated.

Graeme noticed this too and said, "I need to talk to him," which was my cue to leave, but not before firing a parting shot. At some point in the conversation, Jasmine's name had come up again, which caused me to feel a rush of hatred.

As I put Sherwood in my car, I casually stated, "You need to take a baseball bat to *her* head."

Graeme turned back toward me and looked at me with his mouth slightly agape, yet still sizing me up. He was bewildered that I could even suggest such a thing, and I saw a feral protectiveness in his eyes like I had just threatened to take an extremely valuable treasure away from him.

"No, that's not true," was the only response he could muster.

He may have had more to say, but I didn't give him the chance. I climbed into my car and said, "Yeah you do. See you later, Graeme."

I closed the door not knowing that it would be the last time I ever saw him as a free man. The last time I ever spoke with him came ten days later, on March 2nd, 2007. I was at my desk at work, when my cell phone rang, and I could see his number on the call display.

"What's up Graeme?" I answered.

He wasted very little time with small talk before asking, "What are you doing tonight? I've got tickets to the Kings tonight that I want to sell."

"Sorry, I just made plans," I replied. I didn't give him any more details because it was my birthday celebration, and I didn't want him around.

"That's too bad. I could use some money for the weekend," he replied.

"What?!"

"Yeah, my account has been compromised, so it's been deactivated. I have to wait until Monday to get it taken care of."

It's possible that Graeme was telling the truth. With the type of people he had hanging around his house, it's not unbelievable that one of them stole his information and took money out of his account. It's also possible that Ryan was the one who had *compromised* Graeme's account. With no business income, Graeme was almost certainly living off whatever was left of the estate, which Ryan legally owned and was well within his rights to protect.

These possibilities aside, I was alarmed that he had to sell off hockey tickets to have money for the weekend because it indicated that he was now completely broke. In the past, he always had his credit cards or money stashed around the house, but in just six short months of hard living, everything was gone. I had been expecting this collapse to happen, waiting for it even, but it's still surreal when it finally happens. Once I turned him down, he quickly said goodbye and hung up, presumably to try to find another taker for the tickets.

The next week, I called him to see if he had been able to get access to his accounts, but he didn't answer his phone. This was not unusual because he preferred text messaging, so I sent him a text as well. I received no reply, so I tried again the next day with the same result. For a week, I continued to try to reach him, but the texts were never returned and the calls all went straight to voicemail. Since it was apparent that his phone had been permanently turned off, I knew that something was very wrong. I started trying to find out what was going on, and James was one of the first people I called.

"Have you talked to Graeme?" I asked him.

"No, you?"

"There's something going on," I stated, "He's always got that fucking phone with him."

"Maybe we should go over there and see if he's still alive," James suggested, but neither of us really wanted to face the potential danger of going over there. We decided instead to wait and see if someone would contact us, and before long, someone did.

I was sitting in my cubicle when my cell phone rang, but because I could see from the call display that it was Jason from hockey, I didn't answer. I thought that he might be calling to see if I was coming to hockey, which I had no interest in doing. With Graeme out of the picture, the team had become a bunch of individuals hogging the puck, and I was having none of it. I was curious, however, to see if he would leave a message. Fifteen seconds later, the display notified me that I had a new voicemail. Ten seconds after that, I was listening to his message.

"Mike, it's Jason. I'm trying to confirm some information about Graeme," he said with a combination of resignation and disbelief in his voice.

I paused and, for perhaps a minute, stared down at my phone on the desk. As I pressed the buttons to call him back, my heart was racing. I knew that I was about to find out something horrible, and while I had predicted this moment, I still couldn't believe it was happening.

"Hello," he answered.

"Hey, Jason it's Mike. What's going on with Graeme?"

"He shot his son."

News Release
Monday, March 5, 2007

Father and Son Dispute Ends in Murder

Los Angeles: On March 2, 2007, at about 5:00 p.m., Los Angeles Police officers from the West Los Angeles Division responded to a radio call of "Ambulance ADW, Shots Fired" at the 9100 block of Larchmont Circle. When officers arrived at the home they saw the suspect, Graeme Bercham exiting the home yelling for help. Graeme Bercham was taken into custody in the front yard of the home.

Officers entered the home and found the body of 32- year-old, Ryan Bercham with several gun-shot wounds. Paramedics responded and pronounced the victim dead.

Ryan Bercham is the son of the suspect Graeme Bercham. Graeme Bercham was interviewed and booked for Murder. At this time the motive for the shooting is unclear.

CHAPTER 15 – KEEP KEEPING ON

"Hey Dad," Johnathan says as he looks down on me from the loft area just outside of his bedroom.

"Yes?"

"Some guy called about Brian Merchant?"

"Who?" I know a lot of people but Brian Merchant is not one of them.

"He said not to be alarmed."

I have a pretty good idea what this about, and my heart rate begins to increase in response. When I lived in Los Angeles, Sandra and I were still sharing our cell phone account because apparently it's harder to break those contracts than it is a marriage. Finally a couple of years ago, I got my own account and Sandra transferred my number to Johnathan.

I meet him at the bottom of the stairs and pull up his call history. I see two calls from an L.A. area code, so now I definitely know what this is about. Since I discovered that lasd.org inmate locator provides court date information, I have consistently followed the progress of the Graeme's legal proceedings. Each time a new court date scheduled, I take note of when and plan to check again. For the past seven years, as much as 2 months, and few as 2 weeks, have passed between court appearances. In December, I noticed that there was a change in tempo, and the dates had become more frequent. Last time I looked, there were only three days in between. Now this call; it is too much of a coincidence.

I dial the number to the L.A. County District Attorney's Investigations office and let it ring. Voicemail.

"Hi, this is Mike Korkie. I just got your message and am returning your call. I have a new number that you can call me at." I bet myself that this won't take long, and within minutes I'm on the phone with an investigator.

"Sorry about the delay in my response. My son has my old number now, so I'm lucky to have gotten your message at all," I explain. In the last couple of years, several of my friends have thought I must have been mad at them because I never responded to their calls or texts. The fact that I got this message within two days can only have been divine intervention.

"I heard that; I have a teenage son myself. Well listen, I'm calling from the L.A County D.A office about the case of Graeme Bercham. Danette Myers, one of the DA's, would like to talk to you about flying out here to testify. All expenses paid, of course."

"When?"

"His trial starts on Monday so probably later in the week. Is this best number for Danette to reach you?"

A couple of hours later, I am on the phone with D.A Meyers, and she tells me that she is going to need me to testify. I'm not sure how what I know about Graeme is relevant, and I shouldn't be so excited about going back to L.A. for this purpose, but I can't help it. Seven years is a long time to be obsessed with something, but that is exactly what I have been since getting Jason's call.

I sat at my desk that day reading and rereading the article about Ryan Bercham's death. As I tried to process it, my shock that Graeme had killed one of sons was equaled by my confusion. The moment Jason told me, I immediately knew it was Grant because I had witnessed his fury and heard Graeme's stories of his violent aggression. I had known about Grant's constant drug use and how it ignited an already volatile relationship. I guessed that the newspaper had found out that Graeme had two sons and simply put the wrong name in the article. Graeme had alluded to serious problems with Ryan, but they were in the past.

I couldn't have been more wrong, and the outpouring of grief and rage on MySpace in the following months pulled the rest of the picture into focus. Apparently, I was not the first guest in the Bercham home. I met some of the others online, and these people had seen in full view what I had only figured out toward the end. The person that I had thought of as a friend was an abusive monster. While acknowledging that Ryan had been a drug addict, they felt that he was driven to it by his father. Further, the people who loved Ryan and hated Graeme were not particularly surprised. Some went as far to speculate that Julia Bercham's death was not an accidental overdose; rather, it was part of an elaborate plot. Julia was also an addict, an easy target, and they were certain that Graeme was somehow responsible for her death. Ryan had started to assume control of the estate, so Graeme killed him too.

I found all this new information very disturbing, and it confirmed my decision to get away from the nut jobs in Los Angeles. While I waited for the job market to cooperate, I continued to make the best of it through hockey, primarily in Panorama City. Now, the name Panorama City might evoke images of a picturesque, middle class enclave nestled in the Southern California hills. In reality, it is the exact opposite of that. It is a beaten down ghetto located in the heart of the San Fernando Valley that could easily be picked up, dropped into

Mexico City, and not look out of place. The first time James invited me to skate with his team, I drove past the rink five times and never could find it. It was a converted bowling alley that looked nothing like my image of a hockey rink. Often during the 105 degree heat of the summer, the ice would start to turn to slush in long lines down the ice where there was not a pipe directly under to keep it chilled.

Still, it was a better environment than I had left behind in Culver City. I began to make some friends and was invited to join a private pickup every Saturday afternoon. These sessions were the informal practice for the Los Angeles Ice Pirates, a team put together for tournaments in Las Vegas. Each spring and fall we would go to Vegas, play four games in 36 hours, and fit in as much debauchery as our bodies could handle. Of the five that I went to, we won three, got to the finals every time, drank a ton, and even managed to develop an arch rivalry with a team from Anaheim. They claimed to be the best amateur team in SoCal, and we begged to differ. It felt good to get a taste of being part of a travel team – semi-real hockey – and the intensity that goes along with it.

Through this circle of friends I met a woman named Teri, who was also a hockey player. Before long, we moved in together as roommates, and not long after that we were more than roommates. She was exactly what I thought I would have wanted in a woman: easy-going, loyal, hot, hockey player. When it went sideways, it reinforced my resolve that I was done with relationships, and I no longer had any emotional attachment to California. I religiously scoured the internet boards, sent in resumes, and waited for replies. Gradually, I saw some interest and started to field a few calls from recruiters. For months, however, there were no in-person interviews and absolutely no offers.

2007 had been a record year at USH, but our financials began to change right from the beginning of 2008. Initially, it was subtle, but soon the downward trend was clear. Fortunately for me, the job market tends to lag the economy. In July, I met Kyndal and Johnathan at my parent's house in Canmore for a weeklong vacation. While I was there, the CFO of a massive agricultural chemical company called me for a phone interview. It went very well, and I was so excited that I promised Kyndal that I would buy her a cell phone if I got the job.

My mother was quite put off by the notion and exclaimed, "She's eight years old!"

I didn't think it a big deal, and I had an ulterior motive. Being a little superstitious, I thought if I gave Kyndal extra incentive to cheer me on, it could only help my chances. It was exhilarating to be on the verge of finally getting what mattered most to me, and I was amazed to have almost completed all the work that seemed so daunting at my rock bottom. Unfortunately, life often evens itself out. The same day as my interview, I got terrible news. The friends looking after Sherwood called to tell me he had gotten violently ill and passed away. I'm not a religious person, but I really don't think the timing was a coincidence. We travelled a road together, and he had helped me through my most difficult time. Now, his job was done and he is on to whatever is next. I was sad that I couldn't be there for him during his final moments, and I miss him.

Things went quickly after that. I flew to Raleigh, spent the weekend with the kids, and on Monday morning made the ninety minute drive to for a face-to-face interview. It turned out to be for the formality of making an offer, and I was unable to fully contain the jubilation I experienced the moment I understood that I had been hired. The industry and the company couldn't be much less interesting, but the wealth generated from it is. Immediately, I went from scraping by in California to a very comfortable life in North Carolina. The location wasn't exactly what I had hoped, but Raleigh was just never a good place for me. Things hadn't worked out for me there, and it's not surprising that even when everything fell into place Raleigh still didn't really cooperate. I was always swimming against the current in that city; eventually, I had to ease over to the shoreline and accept a slightly different path.

Movers came to my duplex in West L.A., packed up my belongings, and shipped them to Greensboro. I hopped on a plane, showed up for work three days later, and started house shopping. The circumstances of my return were an amazing contrast to my move two and a half years earlier. I had rented a U-Haul and drove every mile of I40 from Raleigh to Barstow in two and half days with no plan for what I would do when I got there.

I don't like to think about what would have happened to my kids and me if I hadn't landed this job because two months later we had the biggest economic bust since the Great Depression. The job market didn't fully recover for another seven years, and who knows when I would have been able to return to North Carolina. I even found out that my position at USH was eliminated soon after I left. In an odd financial quirk, the profits of my new company reached record levels due to the spike in commodity prices. Not only was my job safe all the way through the Great Recession, but the company also continued to give raises and pay bonuses for most of it. I don't know what lies ahead, but that was the most fortunate period of my life.

My career was finally where I hoped it would be, but I was completely starting over from a social perspective. At least when I moved to L.A., George was there, and I met a lot of people through him. Outside of work, I literally didn't know a single person in Greensboro, so as I had in L.A. I went to the rink. It was a much different experience than I expected. For a relatively small southern community, the level of play was very high. There were several players who I found it difficult to keep up with, and I soon found out that these were ex-pros who put down roots in the area after their careers ended. There was even an all-women team in the league, called The Hookers, who seemed worth keeping up with.

Hockey is alive and well in the South, and before long I was skating every week with the North Carolina Eagles, a team formed out of the remnants of the Carolina Thunderbirds ECHL team. Much as it had in L.A. with the Ice Pirates, my circle of friends began to build from hockey, and life settled into a nice rhythm.

My new routine included a 45 minute drive every weekend to a meeting place halfway between Raleigh and Greensboro. Even though Graeme would never take my advice about Jasmine, I took his about Sandra. Over time, the wounds had healed, and she understood that she would never find a man as committed to our kids as I. My presence in North Carolina had proved it to her, and we began a very healthy co-parenting arrangement. Two years later, she moved to Pittsburgh for an accelerated nursing program and felt comfortable(ish) leaving the kids with me for the year. When she moved back to North Carolina, she decided to make Greensboro her permanent home, and we've not looked back. It was a long journey back to raising them fulltime, and it happened in a way that I couldn't even have conceived but did nonetheless.

Throughout this time, I used social media to check on people from my California life, particularly the Berchams. For a year or two, I maintained a presence on both Myspace and Facebook, but gradually I found I was only looking at Myspace to see what information Grant was sharing. Eventually, even that faded away as Graeme's legal proceedings seemed to drone on endlessly. Grant grudgingly made the switch to Facebook about a year after I did, and to my surprise he sent me a friend request.

I thought he would not want to be in contact with me because I had been interviewed by the detectives in Graeme's case and told them everything I knew. The fact that I was cooperating certainly would have been communicated to Grant. I wondered if it might be a case of *keep your friends close and your enemies closer*, and occasionally that concerned me. Even so, I stayed connected with him because I wanted information. While I knew that Grant's version of events could not always be trusted, his posts were a decent source of information on the progress of Graeme's case.

I am also fascinated by Grant's resilience. In the span of fifteen months, he had lost his mother, his older brother, and effectively his father. This type of family devastation could ruin even the most grounded person, and not surprisingly, it was a tumultuous time for him. One week he would be posting about the love of his life; the next he'd be calling the same woman a gold digger. I didn't try to stay current on all the ups and downs of his love life, but in early 2009 there was headline news – Grant's girlfriend was pregnant.

So while Graeme Bercham sat in a jail cell awaiting trial, he was to become a grandfather, in spite of having done almost everything he could to take himself out of the gene pool. He killed one son and so drastically messed up the raising of the other that he was always one mistake away from overdosing. But human genes don't fade away easily, and Grant's girlfriend gave birth to another Bercham boy.

Through social media, I have watched this young man start life, and I hope nothing but the best for him. If anyone has ever had the odds stacked against him, it is Graeme's unfortunate grandson. He seems to have a devoted mom, which will help, but Grant has struggled to stay in his life. On more than one occasion, Grant has posted about being unable to see his son. The root cause is always drug abuse, but fortunately, the mother allows Grant visitation when he gets clean. Currently, Grant is by all accounts sober. He seems quite proud about completing a stint at the Pasadena Recovery Center, run by the most famous of all addiction medicine specialists, Dr. Drew Pinsky. I hope that he sticks with it, but as Dr. Drew points out it takes, on average, five attempts at rehab before it finally works. I'm certain Grant is now well past the average.

Since I know I'm testifying, I wonder if I am going to see him at the courthouse. I don't know what the process is, or if I'll even be allowed to speak with anyone while I'm there. As awkward as it might be, I will try. I have waited long enough, and I want to know what went so terribly wrong that day.

CHAPTER 16 – FIVE SHOTS

A month after Julia passed away on January 17, 2006, Graeme and his two sons took her will to the office of estate attorney Charles Shultz. Everything was split between the sons, leaving nothing to Graeme. The will gave the house on Larchmont Circle to Ryan, and the duplex that Graeme had wanted me to live in was given equally to Ryan and Grant. The gross value of the estate was around $2.4 million in real estate and $50,000 to $75,000 in cash, but there was a mortgage on the house, so the net value was less than $2,000,000. Shultz made it clear the will was not a natural disposition and could be attacked. They all agreed, Graeme included, that it expressed Julia's intentions and no one wished to challenge.

Ryan was named executor of the estate but asked that Shultz communicate through Graeme. It makes sense when one considers that the whole arrangement was conceived by Graeme, and they had a father-son agreement that the estate really belonged to the father. As a part of that agreement,

Graeme would protect it from his bankruptcy, take care of it after that, and then pass it on to his sons when he died. None of them, however, could have predicted how Jasmine Getty would alter Graeme's mental state, and the plan started to unravel.

I suspected that the estate was being drained and mismanaged, and Ryan had spent the better part of a year telling people the same. Several people would later testify that Ryan thought Graeme was quickly burning through money as a result of his lifestyle, and he worried that a significant amount of money was missing from the estate. Ryan was also very well aware of Graeme's drug use and had come to believe that he was an irrational and very angry man. One of the times that Ryan had seemed so rude to me was because he had been humiliated by bounced checks and found out that the mortgage had not been paid for two months. Graeme had recently borrowed $15,000 from family friend Micah Canter, telling Canter that the money was to take care of expenses related to the estate. The house was on the verge of foreclosure, and the volatility of the situation escalated.

In December of 2006, three months before his death, Ryan made a holographic will leaving his interest in Julia's real property to Graeme and his personal property to his boyfriend, Ryan. According to the boyfriend, Ryan said it was Graeme who told him to make the will. Graeme would later deny this claim and assert that Ryan had asked him how to make a will. He took the opportunity to explain that, in absence of a will, were something to happen to Ryan, Graeme would inherit everything. In hindsight, this should have been a red flag, but it does show that there was still a level of trust between them. Few sons would believe that his father would kill him for money, so Ryan had the will drawn up. Presumably, he wanted to ensure that if something happened to him, his personal possessions would go to his boyfriend.

Meanwhile, the probate process was stalled. Schultz made several unsuccessful inquiries to Graeme in an attempt to get values for the property in the estate, which Schultz needed to move the probate process forward. Having spent time with Graeme while he catalogued his art collection, I know that he would have had all that information readily available. He was fastidious with his finances, that is, until Jasmine changed his focus. While Shultz said it was not out of the ordinary for probate to take longer than a year to conclude, there was no reason for Graeme's to expedite the process either. Disclosing the details of property values would only have served to alarm Ryan and cause him to take action much sooner than he did.

Finally, on March 2nd, 2007 at around 1:00 p.m., Ryan phoned Shultz and expressed that he was no longer willing to accept the speed at which things were proceeding. Shultz told

Ryan to come in for a meeting the following Monday, so he could continue the process without having to wait on Graeme. Earlier in the day, Ryan had met Graeme at a bank to sign refinance papers on Larchmont house and also pick up the monthly allowance check Graeme provided while he was attending school. Ryan was aware that Graeme had borrowed money from Canter and decided to confront Graeme about it that morning. Graeme denied that the money was for estate expenses, directly contradicting what he had told Canter.

Over the course of that day, Ryan and Graeme exchanged several text messages and phone calls in which Ryan stated that he was going to get someone else to manage the estate. These communications set in motion the events that led to the shooting because Graeme began to panic. He spoke to Canter on the phone and was very frustrated. Graeme obviously did not believe such drastic action was necessary and asked Canter to speak to Ryan on his behalf. When Canter spoke to him, Ryan confirmed his belief that the estate was in jeopardy and that he would be moving forward with his plan.

At some point, Ryan left a message for his advisor at Loyola Marymount, Father William, saying he was going to stop by Graeme's house to talk to him about his concerns regarding the finances. He also spoke with one of his instructors, Sister Mary, about this visit, and told her he was afraid of Graeme because of his substance abuse issues. He told her that Graeme's behavior was unpredictable and that Ryan never knew what his reactions would be. Ryan had found a stable community of friends and confidants at his school, so he looked to them for guidance. He was uncertain about his decision to talk to Graeme about spending money on drugs and alcohol. Since none of them were aware of the history of violence between the two men, they would have had no idea just how dangerous the situation was.

At 1:30 p.m., LAPD officers went to Graeme's house in response to a report of a *female disturbance.* If it was Ryan who called the police, I'm not sure what he hoped to accomplish, but it angered Graeme. He answered the door and wondered why officers were at the house. He told the officer he was having a problem with his biological ex-son involving probate, but did not mention anything about being threatened. I think it is a reasonable assumption that the ex-son he spoke of was Ryan; however, Graeme would later claim that he was referring to Grant. The officers left the house without incident, and Graeme was free to go about his day, which included using cocaine.

The officers who visited Graeme most likely went to the front door of the house, which entered into a foyer just between Graeme's bedroom and the living room. Almost no one used that entrance, however, because the driveway was on the other side of the house. Most people entered through the side door that led directly into the laundry room. From the small laundry room you could either turn right into the kitchen, or you could go straight into a short hallway that led to my bedroom on the left or the family room straight ahead. Both my bedroom and the family room looked out onto the pool area. The kitchen led to the dining room and, in turn, the living room; all three were street side. The family room and living room shared a wall that divided the house in half, and on the other side of those rooms were the rest of the bedrooms. Graeme did not sleep in the nicer bedroom with the poolside view, but rather chose the one on the corner closest to the street. I suspected that this was simply a carry-over from when he was still cohabitating with Julia but in separate bedrooms.

On one of my last trips back to Graeme's, I parked my car across the street, walked up the driveway to the metal gate between the garage and the house, and entered through the side door. This was my usual path into the house, but I had a very unusual feeling. It was foreboding, like the feeling you get watching a horror movie and you say to the character on the screen about to meet their demise, *Do not go in there*!

The rational part of my brain knew that there was really no great danger for me, but I had fleeting feelings of what it would be like to be hit in the head with a bullet and the devastating impact that would have on the bones of a skull. I'll never forget that feeling and try to keep from dwelling on it, but this was the exact same path Ryan Bercham took during his last moments on the planet.

Ryan went to the dentist that afternoon, leaving the dentist's office between 4:00 and 4:30 p.m. Without delay, he headed to the house as he had told Graeme he would when they spoke earlier. Graeme's elderly cleaning lady, Espiranza, was the only person there when Ryan arrived, and she told him that Graeme and Jasmine would be home soon. They returned at around 4:50 p.m., and Ryan immediately confronted Graeme with a pawn ticket, which showed that Grant had sold Julia's jewelry. This was something of which I was well aware, having been present when Grant stole it out of the storage unit, but Ryan was furious because he had only recently found out and not from Graeme.

After a brief argument during which Ryan apparently threatened Jasmine, Ryan stormed out of the house and drove off in his car, only to return moments later. A neighbor, Clem Hoffman, came home from work at 4:50 or 4:55 p.m., and saw Ryan park his car across the street. Hoffman also noticed that Graeme's car was parked in the driveway. He observed Ryan walking to the house with purpose, and looking determined, which was atypical for him. Ryan had reached his breaking point with the situation and was going after the source of problem.

Without knocking, Ryan entered through the unlocked side door but appeared to the neighbor to be empty-handed as he did so. Whether he would have verbally or physically attacked Jasmine cannot be known because Graeme intercepted him in the dining room. When he heard Ryan return, Graeme had grabbed his .38 semi-automatic from his nightstand but hadn't initially chambered a round. Whatever was said in the ensuing, explosive argument caused Graeme to pull back the slide on his gun and fired an errant shot. Almost immediately, a second shot was fired in close quarters as the two men engaged in a violent struggle. Graeme received a bruising blow to his head from Ryan's elbow while the bullet grazed Ryan's shoulder and chin. Upon being struck in the face Ryan immediately began to retreat into the kitchen toward the side door he entered. Graeme chased him and fired a third shot in the kitchen, which struck Ryan in the back but also caused his gun to jam. This wound was not instantly fatal but likely would have been before long. Ryan continued his retreat out of the house but collapsed in the laundry room.

In the aftermath of the initial struggle, Jasmine was cowering in Graeme's bedroom, but Espiranza heard the shooting and rushed to the dining room as quickly as she was able. Because her health was quite frail, she wasn't exactly sure what she witnessed, but she was certain that she saw Ryan lying on his side with Graeme standing over him. She also thought she saw Graeme holding a yellow gun. In actuality, his weapon was made of blue steel, and such a gun would have appeared dark blue or black to someone with poor eyesight.

When I got right up to the edge of death, I tried to imagine what it would be like. I'm sure Ryan was doing the same while Graeme cleared the jam in his gun. The human mind is an amazing thing, and I believe that even in the heat of this fatal clash he would have been processing exactly what was happening to him. My father was one of the people who pulled me back from my demise; Ryan would have known very clearly that his father was about to kill him. It must have been surreal to see his father walk into to the laundry room and shoot the fourth shot through his left cheek. The bullet exited his right cheek and did not kill him, so Graeme continued. He pulled the trigger one final time and sent a bullet into the front part of Ryan's left ear, lodging in his brain and killing him instantly.

Graeme then checked for a pulse and called 9-1-1. He spoke with the dispatcher for just over a minute-and-a-half., and police arrived within the next five minutes. From outside the house, Hoffman had heard three gunshots in rapid succession, about a minute of silence, then two more gunshots. Hoffman's timeline was confirmed by two other witnesses, who were working at nearby properties. One was in close enough proximity to hear a heated argument between two men before the gunshots. The witnesses told the police that there were shots fired inside, which prompted them to order everybody out of the house. As the police were preparing to make a tactical entry, Graeme, Jasmine, and Espiranza came out of the house voluntarily.

Jasmine was hysterically screaming and pointing at Graeme, "Help us, he shot him, he shot him!"

Graeme was crying but was able to say, "Just help him. Help him."

I'm not sure Graeme was crying about his dead son. It may have occurred to him in that moment just how quickly the supposed love of his life turned on him. There was never any doubt who shot Ryan, but Graeme claimed that he did it to defend himself and Jasmine. She, however, made no mention of Ryan trying to hurt them. He killed his own son for her, but all she wanted known very quickly and clearly was that she had nothing to do with it. She is nothing if not an expert in self-preservation.

Because he felt that he had just committed a justifiable homicide, Graeme was cooperative. He let the officers know that the gun he used was inside the house, but that he had a .22

caliber magazine in his pocket. He told them that he had previously removed the magazine from a .22 pistol after receiving threats from Ryan in order to ensure the pistol wasn't used against anyone in the house.

Officers then entered the house and found Ryan lying on his back in the laundry room area, with blood pooling from his head. As he said it would be, Graeme's gun was on the kitchen floor about two feet from Ryan's body, and the trail that led up to the gun told police the story. Bullet fragments and an expended shell casing were found in the dining room. The refrigerator and a kitchen window had bullet holes in them and a second casing was underneath a nearby dog bed. A third casing was found underneath Ryan's lower left back, and the remaining casings were found in the laundry room. There was also a mallet in his right hand, which had a bloody towel lying on top of it. Graeme told police the towel had fallen on Ryan's hand after he became physically sick while checking for a pulse.

By 5:30, within 30 minutes of the shooting, Graeme was arrested and taken to county jail for further questioning. He was charged with first-degree murder with special circumstances. The special circumstances made the death penalty an option, and also meant that he could not be released on bail. It was an abrupt, profound change for a man who had been living high and on the edge for the better part of a year, and he wouldn't taste freedom again for another three years.

CHAPTER 17 – TESTIFY

As I navigate the ten minutes between my house and the parking lot of the Greensboro Airport, I am a little nervous. It has been a couple of years since my last flight. It was an unpleasant work trip from Greensboro to Minneapolis to meet the woman who had taken over our group. I was not getting good feelings from her or my previous boss, and she turned out to be an asshole. To add to my anxiety the flight was easily the most turbulent I had ever experienced. We were either in, or just barely above the clouds the whole way, and when we finally descended we came down fast and hard. I made it safely only to find out that she didn't want me on her team.

When I lived in Los Angeles, I had to fly regularly. I noticed that sometime around late 2007 the airlines seemed to figure out their booking algorithms. Since that time, every flight I've been on has been fully booked. Between bumpy, crowded flights, the extra fees, and the constant delays I resolved to drive anywhere feasible. Driving to testify at Graeme's trial is not feasible, so I hope this trip is smooth. The parking, check-in, and security in Greensboro usually take about fifteen minutes, and today is no different. Good weather, a smooth takeoff, and a couple of cocktails help me ease back into the flying game.

So far so good, but there has been minimal communication from Los Angeles. Neither Danette Meyers nor her support staff has contacted me directly; all I have received is an electronic confirmation of my ticket and hotel address. It is surprising to me that they are not being more proactive, especially since they are pursuing the death penalty. I cannot imagine that I would be the first or last witness to miss their flight or bail out last minute. I guess they figure I'm a grown up and will be there as promised.

Typically, when I returned from North Carolina after a visit, I would land at LAX in the dark. My visits were short, so every second was precious, which meant I usually waited until around 8:00 PM (ET) to leave Raleigh. The circumstances of this trip are obviously much different – I have to take off both Thursday and Friday for a single day of testimony. Leaving early Thursday seems to make the most sense, but it's a bit of a nuisance because I have plans for most of my available vacation time.

Danette has mentioned that she may have to hold me over to Monday, which would mean having to take at least another day off. I have a new job at Greensboro's most successful logistics company, and they didn't get that way by being employee friendly. They pay even better than the agricultural chemical company but are much more restrictive with time off. I hope it doesn't come to that and choose to focus on the unusual opportunity to appreciate the Southern California scenery in the light of day.

We are still at full cruising altitude when I see the outskirts of the L.A. metropolitan area, so I search for places I recognize. The first thing I notice is I-15 dropping down out of the San Gabriel Mountains. Even though it's an Interstate, it's a hair-raising route I took many times, starting with my first trip across the country, and then later, for the Vegas hockey weekends. A few minutes later, I try to see if I can identify the hotel in Ontario where I stayed on my first night in California. It had been midnight, and I just couldn't handle another hour and half to get to George's.

Soon, downtown comes into view and I spot The Standard Hotel, at which I spent a really fun evening on the top floor bar with the finance group at USH. Scanning further to the north, I see the Hollywood sign and not far from that I can make out my old apartment building. All of these landmarks evoke pleasant memories of a life that I have fully left behind. My jitters fade, and the rest of the flight is so smooth I barely pay attention to the landing.

The terminal feels familiar, and I easily make my way to the rental car shuttle. As I move outside of the secure area, my mind goes on alert. Presumably, my testimony will support the prosecution theory of murder for financial gain and land my former friend on Death Row. I wonder if it is worth it for him to somehow communicate with his thug crew and have me taken out before I ever make it to court. I couldn't be an easier target; the District Attorney's office has barely communicated with me, let alone protected me. The rational part of my brain tells me that there is no danger, but on the other hand, L.A. is one of the worst run jurisdictions in the country. Not only would its bureaucrats not know if there was any danger to me, they probably would also not give a fuck. Just another production line murder case to investigate and prosecute. Next.

In spite of my paranoia, I get on the shuttle in search of my rental car and within a half hour I'm navigating to the Ramada Plaza. One major change since I left town is the smart phone. No more getting turned around on L.A. roads; Google Maps seamlessly guides me through the ten minute route. I arrive at the hotel, park, and walk into the renovated lobby. It's quite nice, but like most buildings in Southern California it's a half step off of what it could be. Whether it's the unskilled labor or the crushing costs of real estate, construction is seldom done correctly. Corners are always cut in some way, and it leaves one with the impression of mediocrity.

There is no one else in the lobby, so I walk directly up the desk.

The concierge asks, “Can I help you?”

“Checking in Mike Korkie.”

I don’t want to give him any extra information if I don’t need to, especially if there’s a chance someone might overhear. I assume that the reservation is under my name, but I also suspect that the D.A.s office books many out-of-town witnesses here. Once he finds my reservation, he looks up at me in a way that tells me he knows why I’m here. He wouldn’t have been given any details; nevertheless, it makes me feel self-conscious that he knows I’m a prosecution witness.

The whole process takes less than two minutes before he tells me, “You’re all set.”

With cardkey in hand, I walk twenty feet and enter the waiting elevator. When the door opens at my floor, I see that my room is on the level with outdoor pool and courtyard. It is quiet – too quiet to feel comfortable. If Graeme does have the resources to have me taken out, there will be no witnesses in this hotel. Perhaps because it’s Thursday afternoon, but it doesn’t seem like a hotel this close to LAX should ever be this quiet, especially poolside on a 90 degree day. I make it to my room without incident, however, and get unpacked.

The room is a suite with nice furniture but as usual, just a little off. If you're going to paint, tile, and put in new bathrooms, why wouldn't you finish the job? Don't leave crappy $5 brass knobs on the bathroom door, and don't keep the sixty-year-old windows. Eventually, my mind gets past all the problems, and I relax and watch TV.

At about 5:00 PM, my cell phone rings and I answer, "Hello."

"Hi is this Mike?"

"It is."

"Hi Mike, this is Danette Meyers." Finally, my participation in the trial is at least being acknowledged. "Did everything go well with your trip?"

I can't help but wonder what would happen if it hadn't. Do all their witnesses receive such leeway on their appearance, or have I flown all the way across the country for next to nothing? After the small talk, we make arrangements to meet at her office at the courthouse around 8:30 AM. She is due in court by 9:00, so she will need some time to debrief me before she goes in.

Until then, I am on my own. By the time I eat dinner at the hotel restaurant, make a few phone calls, and watch TV, it is time for bed. When I had first pulled into the hotel parking lot, I noticed a Denny's across the street. I decided that I would get breakfast there before walking over to the courthouse.

In the morning when I enter the busy restaurant, I quickly realize that the best thing to do is sit at the counter. Within minutes, I'm enjoying an omelet and taking in my surroundings. One of the signs on the walls stands out immediately: PEANUT ALLERGY ALERT. The fact that a Denny's feels the need to post such a thing is an unambiguous reminder of where I am and how little I miss living here. Perhaps Californians should stop using so much hand sanitizer, and maybe their immune systems will recover to the point that they can risk exposure to the heinous and deadly peanut.

I finish my food, pay, and begin my walk to court. It is less than a mile, so I only have about ten minutes to reflect on what is about to happen. I am going to see Graeme Bercham for the first time since we went to Aqua nightclub almost seven years ago. While I walk freely down a residential street on a beautiful Southern California day, he is confined to the bowels of Los Angeles County Airport Branch Courthouse. I walk up to the attractive, glass façade building still thinking about what is at stake, and I decide not to dwell on the fact that Graeme could be put to death. I will simply answer all questions truthfully and walk away with a clear conscience. After all, I tried many times to pull him back from the path he was on, but he would hear none of it. His own arrogance has put him in this situation, and even if he is acquitted he has cost himself at least seven years of his life in a correctional facility.

Once I clear security, I feel a sense of relief. My thoughts of Graeme having me killed were unfounded; all the same, a little more communication would have been nice. I ride the elevator to the District Attorney offices, and as I'm preparing to deal with the security officer behind Lexan glass, I see a familiar looking figure. The detective who originally interviewed me, Tony Umansky, is pulling a stack of boxes and walking the same direction. Back then, he gave me his business card, and I have tried on a couple of occasions to call the number it provided. Apparently, shortly after the Bercham murder, he moved on from homicide to become a full-time D.A. investigator.

This is the first time I have spoken with him since he came to my apartment. When I first met him, he seemed suspicious and standoffish. Perhaps he didn't think I would be cooperative and that he was going to have to be forceful. Now, he realizes that I'm fully cooperative and his demeanor is completely different.

"Korkie?"

"That's me," I say as I change directions slightly and reach out my hand to shake his.

"Hey buddy, how are you doing?"

"Great thanks," I reply as he guides me through the secured door and back into the offices.

"Thanks for coming out for this; I know it's a long trip. Where are you now?"

"North Carolina."

"How do you like it out there? You trying to get back here?"

What a question; I had never even considered that someone might think that. When I compare the life I have crafted for myself now to what I had when I lived here, moving back is an impossibility. Instead of taking an hour to get anywhere, it takes me fifteen minutes to everywhere. Most things cost half as much as in California. When people renovate, they can afford to do it right. Graffiti is the exception not the rule.

I could tell him this and more but limit my response to, "No, it's a very happy time for me right now."

As he leaves me alone at a table in the break room, I can tell that he can't fathom why I prefer North Carolina to Los Angeles. I guess people can adapt to almost anything, but I would never willingly go back. The state of California has allowed itself to become like a third world nation. There is a significant wealthy class, a rapidly shrinking middle class under tremendous pressure, and a huge population of people living below or near the poverty line. It's too bad that the idiots who move there for the weather don't realize that there is more to life than not having to put on a jacket year-round.

Before long, a heavy-set, black woman comes into the break room and introduces herself as Danette Meyers. She brings me into her office and begins going through my testimony, which turns out to be about twenty questions related to money Graeme spent on trips, drugs, and Jasmine's dog.

When she is done, I ask, "That's it?"

"I'm really limited in what I can ask you," she confirms with a hint of distaste in her voice. "They've done everything they can to keep what you know out, but we did manage to get some of it in."

Many of the court dates that I noticed on lasd.org were hearings to determine admissibility of evidence. It seems that most of what I know about Graeme and his activities leading up to Ryan's death are not deemed relevant to his murder trial, so I've travelled cross-country for thirty minutes worth of testimony. It reminds me that, when the American government or one of its agencies goes after someone, no expense or inconvenience is spared. Its resources are limitless and hope that you never, rightly or wrongly, wind up in their crosshairs.

With my preparation complete, Umansky takes me to an attractive waiting area with a floor to ceiling view of the city and hills to the north. I miss the wide open vistas that one seldom sees along the eastern seaboard. There are only terrazzo tile benches to sit on, but nevertheless it is a pleasant place to wait. While I do, I look for family and associates of Graeme's but see no one I recognize. Slowly, the activity around the double doors to Graeme's courtroom builds, and I observe what I surmise to be the jury milling about. When the attorneys arrive, the small crowd files into the courtroom. I wonder if perhaps Grant and the other spectators went in before I got to the lobby, but that seems unlikely. It occurs to me that maybe nobody is coming to watch Graeme fight for his life.

For two hours, I enjoy the natural light and contemplate how a man completely destroyed his life. Eventually, I see a first and then a second witness go into Graeme's courtroom. I don't know either of them. When the second reemerges, it doesn't take long for Umansky to follow, "You're up."

I walk past him as he holds the door for me and, for a moment, I lose my bearings. I try to maintain my pace as my eyes adjust to the darkness of the chamber, but I have to slow slightly to find my way past the back row of spectator seating. By the time I make it to the aisle that takes me up to the witness stand, I can see clearly again and start to assess my surroundings. I walk past the rest of the wooden benches and notice that they are completely empty. Not a single person representing Graeme or his dead son has come to watch. I continue toward the witness stand where the lighting is better. A very nice room, it would be considered warm and inviting if the circumstances weren't so ugly.

I still can't identify Graeme because everyone at the tables has their back to me. I notice that the judge and jury are not making eye contact with me. I find that briefly distracting and don't locate Graeme until I'm in the witness box. As I swear to tell the whole truth, I finally get a good look at the man. We make eye contact for about two seconds before he breaks off and looks down at the table in front of him. His expression seems to be a mix of disappointment and embarrassment. I imagine that mine is somewhat similar, but my adrenaline is pumping far too quickly to know for sure.

I fixate on him for a moment and realize that his suit looks like it is hanging off a coat hanger. When I last saw him, his weight seemed about right for his frame, perhaps carrying a little extra belly fat. Now, he looks like he has lost twenty-five pounds and is probably ten pounds underweight. Yet, he looks much better than he did at the height of his cocaine use. His hair is combed, his eyes are no longer bugging out of his head, and his skin has returned to a healthy color.

Danette begins to go through the same questions that she asked me in her office, but this time she is quickly stopped. I recognize Graeme's lawyer Riley, who just finished objecting to the third question. He looks the same as he did when he tracked me down at the rink five years earlier, and I wonder if he's still playing there. I know that it has to be a decent sign for Graeme's financial situation that he has the resources to keep the same legal team from arrest to trial. Either, he hasn't gone through the entire estate, or he has a financial benefactor paying his legal fees. Facing the death penalty with a public defender would be a guaranteed ticket to the gurney, and I'm glad that this is at least a fair fight. Graeme has always claimed that he killed Ryan in self-defense, and I would like the jury to hear his side of the story presented in a competent manner.

Based on Umansky's reaction to the objection, he does not agree. I surmise that Riley must have been a thorn in the side of the prosecution team because Umansky makes no attempt to hide his disdain as he leans back in his chair and rolls his eyes. It is an unprofessional, but honest reaction that I cannot be the only one to notice. It is somewhat understandable given that they've been doing battle for years, but I sense a genuine hatred and wonder what Umansky would do to Riley if he thought he could get away with it.

The judge overrules the first objection, so Danette and I continue with our rehearsed examination, only to be interrupted several more times. In spite of Riley's efforts, I am allowed to answer all the questions I have been prepared for, notwithstanding a rephrasing or two. When she is done, the judge asks the defense team if they have any questions for me. Graeme and Riley confer for about thirty seconds before Riley rises from his chair holding his legal pad. He steps out from behind their table but does not approach past the front of it.

"When you moved in to Graeme's home, there were two of you correct?" he asks.

"No, it was just me," I respond with slight confusion.

"Are you sure?" he presses.

"Yes."

Finally, he decides to spell it out for me, "Sherwood?"

"OH. Yes." I take a moment to collect my thoughts, and with a slight smile turn to the jury, "my dog Sherwood was with me."

There is more that I want to say. For a brief instant, I think about mentioning that Sherwood had died so that Graeme would know, but I stop myself. I realize that it would be inappropriate, and more importantly, Graeme probably wouldn't care. I turn back to Riley to find out where he is going with this.

"No further questions," he declares.

Of all the ways that I had envisioned the cross-examination would go, a single question about my dead dog was not on the list. The judge dismisses me, so I exit the witness box and start walking down the aisle out of the courtroom. I am still processing what happened as I glance over at Graeme for the last time. Umansky hops up from the table and follows me out.

When we get out to the lobby, he says, "Good job. Just hang here for a few minutes."

Shortly thereafter, Umanksy, Meyers, and the jury are released for lunch. The three of us let the jury move away and begin talking as we head to the elevators. We are all somewhat surprised about the lack of cross-examination.

"They were afraid of you," Danette explains.

"You think so?" Even as I ask the question I am skeptical. Riley made it pretty clear when we met that he didn't see any relevance to my testimony. I'm certain, if he wanted to, he could have asked a few questions that further minimized my impact. It is clear to me why they only asked about Sherwood; Graeme was sending a message. He wanted to remind me that he had treated my dog and me very well, and I repaid him by testifying against him.

I change the subject slightly and say, "I can't believe that there were no spectators."

Umansky gets a dry smile on his face and replies, "It's not like downtown with the high profile cases."

His words put the ruined life of Graeme Bercham into perspective. The California criminal justice system can be glamourous in a twisted way. It brings to mind names like O.J.

Simpson, Charles Manson, Phil Spector, as well as the morbid curiosity created by their trials. Many times, I have searched for a news story about Graeme's case and have found nothing. Where I grew up, a high profile member of the hockey community murdering his oldest son would be talked about for years, but in Los Angeles, California it is less than a blip. Graeme has reduced himself to the level of tens of thousands of other criminals battling for their freedom in complete obscurity.

As we part ways, Danette thanks me for my participation and explains where I can go to get my expense paperwork taken care of. We shake hands she leaves me with one final thought, "He's pure evil. He executed his own son."

I can tell that she believes her statement without a shred of doubt, and I wonder if she will be able to convince the jury. I will spend some time pondering that as I prepare to reconnect with old friends. I walk back to the hotel and start texting people I hope to see this weekend. Within an hour, it's clear that everyone but James has other plans, so around six I make the one hour drive into The Valley to hang out with James, his wife Chauntel, and their baby daughter.

We have a nice sushi dinner, compliments of Los Angeles County, and then go back to their apartment for drinks and conversation. Chauntel sets the baby on top of kitchen table as we sit and talk. I instinctively put my hand on her lower back to keep her from falling off. It makes me a little uncomfortable that she is up there, and it occurs to me that I am the most experienced parent in the room. I often hear people with older children say they miss the baby years and have always dismissed that. I've happily moved out of Babytown, and I'm at teenage junction with Empty Nest City in sight. But for the first time in a long while, I am around a baby and quite enjoying it.

Before long, James asks me if I want to go outside for some air, which in California means, *let's go smoke*.

I accept, in spite of my employer's alleged random drug testing policy, and we go downstairs. For the twenty years that I've worked in professional environments, random has always meant, *once*, before you're officially hired. Weed is not nearly as accessible in North Carolina as it is in California, so I haven't partaken many times since 2008. I decide that the garden of James' apartment complex is a good place to do so again.

"So what's up with you and this Dawn Anne? Are you dating her, or what?" James asks after he finishes lighting up his joint.

"Who?"

I see the confused look on his face that I had hoped for. It is a gag that I have been enjoying for the past five years. Dawn was one of The Hookers, and I met her during my first Greensboro league game. Our team was short of players, and Dawn was always hanging around the rink looking for free ice time. I was mildly impressed that she scored that day, but I didn't really get to know her until we started dating a year later. It was casual, and I had no intention of having a relationship, with her or anyone. Teri complained about the walls I put up, but over time Dawn has insisted on chipping away at them. Pretending I don't know who she is when people ask about her is probably one of those walls. Nevertheless, it is working for us and she is a big reason Sandra's year away at nursing school went smoothly.

James only knows Dawn from our interactions on Facebook, which give people a hint that we are a couple, but there is room for doubt. After a couple more moments of deadpan, I acknowledge what my friends in Greensboro already know, that we are living together in a committed relationship. James isn't the first person to fall for it and won't be the last; it never gets old. I even did *Who*? at my brother's wedding and almost gave my Aunt Broyna a heart attack, thinking she had been calling her the wrong name all day.

About an hour later, I say goodnight to everyone and then make the trip south on the 405 back to my hotel, knowing I'll be coming back the opposite direction in the morning. I've always loved this drive, especially when the traffic is light. I climb up the Santa Monica Mountains and then begin the steep drop down the other side passing familiar landmarks such as the Skirball Center, UCLA, and the Getty Museum, as well as less famous places like George's old apartment. Another fifteen minutes, and I am in my hotel room looking forward to the morning. James and I are going to play in the Saturday pickup for the first time in several years. It is no longer an Ice Pirates pickup – the team folded around 2010 – but it is still run by former Pirate, Pierre. Just before I moved away, he told me that I was always welcome to play when I was in town. As soon as I knew that I could stay the weekend, I reached out and took him up on his offer.

* * *

It feels good to be in the dressing room, but it seems that I am not the only person who has moved on from our weekly ritual. I had thought that I would be earning enough at my new job to make a point of flying to LA at least a couple of times a year. I did make it for one final Vegas tournament in 2008, but this is my first time back to Los Angeles. Of the five or six faces I recognize, like Mike our Vegas goalie, at least half are here because I let them know I would be coming. It was a fun group back then: Todd, Guy, Big Rob, Dave, Daniel, Teri and several others. None of them are here today.

Unlike the turnout, the ice does not disappoint; it is exactly as I remember. The blistering hot weather outside is causing little puddles of standing water all over rink. In spite of the ice conditions, I make sure I appreciate the experience. There is nothing like ninety minutes of hockey to pause the world for a little bit, no matter where you are. The level of hockey, while not what it used to be, is still pretty good. They have picked up some new guys who can fly, but I've been keeping in shape and hold my own. Afterward in the dressing room, Mike comments that I don't look like I've lost a step, which I take as high praise. We have some beers and take some pictures for posterity. I take my time before saying my goodbyes because I know that this will be the last time I ever play here.

As I set out down the 405, the traffic is much heavier than last night, but I have given myself a lot of time to drop the rental car and shuttle at the airport. When I finally get to the airport exit, it takes me past one of the lots I used to use for LAX parking, and my subconscious reaction is immediate. The most stressful part of my trips to Raleigh was finding and paying for parking. It was always in the dark, I was always tired, and it cost fifty bucks I didn't have. Like everything in L.A., it is more difficult and twice as expensive as in Greensboro. It puts me on edge as I return the rental car, take the shuttle to the terminal, and make my way to my gate.

As I board the flight and take my seat, I'm hoping the flight home is as relaxing as the one that brought me here. Most times that I've flown out of LAX, it feels like being shot out of a cannon over the Pacific. Then once at an altitude of 10,000 feet, the plane quickly turns 180 degrees back toward the east. It can be tough on a white knuckle flyer, but this time we take an unusual route that I find even more intense. We take off to the north over the Hollywood hills and then through the peaks of the San Gabriel Mountains. For several minutes, I lean into every twist and turn while watching out my window. The view is impressive but all I can think is, "Climb baby climb!" Finally, we clear the last of the mountains and level off.

I feel much better.

CHAPTER 18 – A VERY NICE HAT

The text reads, "I think I got Hamrlik."

I am perplexed so I respond back, "what do you mean?"

"I think I've got Hamrlik for Florida."

"Roman Hamrlik?"

"Yes," comes his final reply because as soon as I see it, I immediately call my friend Chowder.

"How do you know Roman Hamrlik?" I ask the gigantic ex-East Coast Hockey league player, who is helping me put together this year's edition of the North Carolina Eagles. Now that my part in Graeme's trial is over, I am back to focusing on my annual trip down to Florida for the USA Hockey National Championship. The organization has been travelling to the Nationals since 1987, winning a total of six. It is a tight group, and my experience with them has been radically different than it was playing for Graeme, who accepted me into his home and his life after a mere four games.

Minor league hockey doesn't pay well, but often the players make connections, put down roots, and start careers in their post hockey lives. The Eagles formed out of the remnants of the ECHL's Carolina Thunderbirds, and they are a family that doesn't easily accept outsiders. They started off in the open division and have stayed together as time has taken them through several USA Hockey age brackets. It took me a full season of skating with them before I got to know them at all. They were aging out of the Over 40 level, and they felt that I could provide some young legs. We didn't come close to winning that year, but I played well and we partied hard. Over time, I have taken on a bigger role, and most of the core group has moved on to the Over 50 division. Unfortunately, the transition has been tough, and the organization is in the midst of a seven-year drought.

One of the few Eagles originals left behind is Bob, or as we often call him, Bobby Two Scoops. He gets that name from the mysterious concoction of powder that he mixes into his pre-game drink. If it's an important game, he needs at least two scoops to get ready. His intensity makes him the heart and soul of the team, but in the past he has had to sit out when the rest of his teammates moved to a new age bracket. For the past four years, we've been trying to build a new generation of the Eagles. Our cobbled together rosters have resulted in us being badly outmatched on many occasions. As Bob so succinctly put it, we've been bringing a knife to a gunfight.

Now Chowder has gotten involved, and it seems that this might finally be our year. "This Czech kid, Petr, I coached in college was best friends with Hamrlik growing up. Well he's not a kid anymore obviously, but he's still a kid to me, y'know? Anyway, Petr wants to play, so he's trying to convince Hamrlik,"

"That would be awesome, but I'll believe it when I see it," I counter, and I have good reason to be skeptical. Every year, we check in with local NHLers to see if they are interested in coming down to play, only to hear shortly thereafter that they can't do it.

Nevertheless, it's hard not to get excited about the way this year's roster is coming together. We've been recruiting hard and have several strong commitments. In the small world category, the manager of the Panorama City rink, Jocelyn, has moved to North Carolina too. He played in the southern minor leagues and decided to move his family back in search of better opportunities. Adding Roman Hamrlik – and his 1400 games of NHL experience – to a team with seven pro and three varsity college players could finally be enough to push us over the top.

I try not to get too far ahead of myself because recruiting players is only one of many things needed for a successful tournament. I still must finish registering the team, arranging for our jerseys, negotiating a group rate at the beach hotel, and collecting the money. Last but not least, I need to continue getting myself in shape. I am glad for all the distractions because I fully expect this phase of Graeme's legal proceeding to drag on like everything else. It would be nice to get closure, and even though I know his chances of freedom are slim, I still have trepidation about the outcome. We were friends, and I testified against him; would he become a threat to me or my family if he was found not guilty and released? I wouldn't put anything past a man who shot his son in the back, including winning his freedom again.

For seven years I have had nothing to worry about from Graeme. In the immediate aftermath of his arrest, he was only a threat to himself. He was put on suicide watch, and then there certainly would have been a period of cocaine withdrawal that would have kept him from being fully functional. Once he recovered and accepted his situation, however, he started fighting for his life. Given his level of narcissism, he would not mind being caged up for the rest of his life if the alternative was to die strapped to a gurney. So, his strategy became very simple: delay. He was once again an attorney, with nothing but available time to focus on the case and, quite literally, a lot of skin in the game.

From 2007 to 2010, Graeme and his attorney ground the case to a halt with pre-trial motions, the most successful being to suppress the evidence collected from his house. He argued that because it was collected without a search warrant, it was inadmissible. When the first responding officers entered his home, they did so because they reasonably believed that someone inside the home needed aid. They did an initial sweep of the house and determined that, other than the body of Ryan Bercham, it was empty. With the crime scene secured, they arrested Graeme and transported him to jail. Detectives and photographers then entered the house and began their investigation. The trial judge agreed with Graeme and ruled that only evidence visible in plain view during the initial sweep was admissible.

This ruling actually forced the prosecution to drop the charges and release him, but the victory and his freedom were short lived. The charges were quickly refiled and Graeme was arrested outside of the courthouse. This counterpunch by the prosecution allowed them to not only keep him in custody, but it also gave them time to appeal the trial judge's decision. Eventually, an appeal court ruled that because the police maintained an uninterrupted presence in the residence a search warrant was not necessary. Further, requiring the first wave of responders to seize evidence was unreasonable and would have made the operation even more potentially dangerous. In the end, all evidence collected was admitted, with the exception of a hidden bullet fragment.

Ultimately, the prosecution had prevailed, but it had taken another two years. The entire process cost the State of California five years, great expense, and it played into Graeme's strategy of dying of natural causes. If the verdict is guilty and the punishment is death, he will begin the appeals process, which is certain to take years more. California has not put anyone to death since 2006, and there are 754 inmates on death row. Graeme is 65 years old, and there could easily be twenty years of delays. I don't know what his fate is, but I'm quite certain that it is not the death penalty.

I check for updates daily, half expecting to see on Grant's Facebook that the judge has declared a mistrial, but finally there is news of a verdict. On February 2nd, 2014, my daily check of the lasd.org website tells me there has been a guilty verdict in the trial. I immediately navigate to Facebook and see the following message:

> Grant - Guilty First Degree Murder Is the verdict in my fathers trial... I'm at a loss for words I don't know how to feel right now...

I don't know exactly what to feel either; I am relieved but also have sympathy for Grant. He has now officially lost his entire family of origin. By many accounts, his was a difficult childhood, but I did see love between Graeme and his son. He is almost as much a victim in all of this as his brother, and immediately there are messages of support from his friends who understand.

> Dina - I'm so sorry, Grant.
> George Z - Oh My God Grant. I am so sorry.
> Hiilary P - please feel free to call me if you want ill inbox you my number...we are here for you okay

For a couple of days, many positive messages follow. Regrettably, as so often happens on social media, the positivity fades and arguments erupt. I could have predicted disagreements between Graeme supporters and Ryan supporters, but I really didn't expect fights between Grant's sober friends and his party friends.

> Thad B - We need to have beers Grant and talk about this shit. Hit me up
> Lindsay B - Yeah! Drink up! Great advice......you fucking idiot. Invite a grieving alcoholic/addict out to get wasted and wallow in self-pity, shame and sadness. He's not suffering enough already, right? Let's throw some gas on that fire!
> Hannah - Acceptance isn't the easiest medicine to swallow but it is the best for you
> Lindsay B - But beers taste so much better than acceptance!
> Thad B - Thanks mom.
> Nicole - You'd think some of you would practice being tactful, and find a better time and place to call people names and argue about stupid shit on Facebook. Because I'm sure Grant really wants to be reading comments in this post and see his friends arguing on Facebook. Grow up people and have some respect.

To his credit, Grant does not engage in any of the negativity and he simply posts:

Grant - Thanks everyone for your support.

Before long, lasd.org and Grant's timeline inform me that Graeme is to be sentenced March 24th. The jury will decide between life in prison with no chance of parole, or if they are unanimous, the death penalty. They had gone into their deliberations with the options of first or second degree murder, voluntary manslaughter, and not guilty. They were initially split 10-2 in favor of first-degree murder, and shortly thereafter, the holdouts were swayed to a unanimous verdict. In six weeks, they will be brought back together to finish their job.

* * *

My phone vibrates on my bedside table waking me up and indicating I have a message. My alarm for work has not yet gone off, so either I forgot to set it or it's early. Unsurprisingly, it's another 5am workout video from Bob, which he has been regularly sending the team. This one is of him deadlifting roughly 400lbs, and it almost motivates me to get out of bed a little early and do a few pushups. The 500lb squat video from last week caused a flurry of comments admonishing him not to injure himself before the tournament.

“Jesus Christ Bobby, it hurts me just to watch that,” was one of the responses that pretty much summed up how I felt about it.

For better or for worse, it will be the last inspirational video that we get for a while because April 5th is finally upon us. Bob and I have typically carpooled down to the nationals, and this year is no different. I spend a distracted day at work and then Dawn and I drive over to Bob’s house to meet up with the rest of our traveling group. She has been coming down through the tough years, and refuses to miss this year. She knows how close we are, and the fact that Hamrlik played for her favorite team, the Islanders, doesn’t hurt either. We also have Rich and Brian, so we cram five of us, plus all our gear, sticks, and team jerseys into Bob’s Suburban.

We decided a couple of weeks ago to take the Atlanta route down to Tampa, so we can stop for the night at my brother’s house, which is about the halfway point. Breaking up the eleven hour drive is best if you can, and it’s nice to spend an evening drinking at the lake. It turns out that one of Owen’s shady neighbors is storing a whole bunch of high quality booze in his basement, which is a mistake with this crew. Bob quickly locates the Gentlemen Jack, I find the best tequila, and the party is on. Owen breaks out his guitar and spends the rest of the night playing snippets of songs. Any more than that would require people that could actually carry a tune, but we have fun and still manage to get to bed at a reasonable hour.

We are a little groggy when we wake up in the morning, but nothing some coffee and a hearty breakfast can't fix. By 10 AM, we're on the road, and much of the trip is spent strategizing and planning the lines. There are also nervous text messages flying back and forth regarding travel progress. We already know that Al, one of our new pros, can't make the first game. With nine forwards and five defensemen on the roster, being down one player is not a problem, but we need everyone else. Throughout the day, positive reports trickle in, including one from Chowder, letting us know that Petr and Roman are in Tampa and ready to play. I still have to see it to believe it, but it is great news to start the weekend.

Unfortunately, we soon find out that Owen has been called back for the day to deal with a work emergency. This is not good news, especially considering our first opponent, Famous Joe's Pizza. From Huntsville Alabama, their players are mostly alumni of that city's NCAA and minor pro teams. They are the two time defending champion and have beaten us every time out. On a personal level, my physical battles with this team have gone far beyond typical adult league competition.

Apparently at some point early in the six years that I've been coming to this tournament, I hurt one of their players with an aggressive play. At the time, the player was on a different team, so I didn't make a connection between the hit and Famous Joe's. He never forgot and definitely didn't forgive, so two years ago in what was an elimination game for us, they evened the score. I initially didn't realize what was happening, but once they got up by six goals, it quickly became clear that they were after me. Every time I was on the ice, one or more of them was trying to take me out. Fortunately for me, they had to try to do it within the adult non-check rules. Unfortunately, at that level, the refs give a lot of leeway, and there is a lot you can get away with. Worse yet, that was our most disjointed team ever, so I didn't even know half of our players. The guys I did know had no idea there was a problem.

I haven't had players come at me that hard since my days of full contact hockey, and I don't think I've ever had a whole team come at me with no backup from my own team. After the game when Bob found out what had happened, he asked why I didn't tell him. Mostly it was because I thought he knew, but in the heat of battle I also didn't feel like running to anyone for help. I took everything they had and gave back everything I had, including a couple of world class chops. By the end of the game, I had a sore knee and a simmering rage, but as is customary I looked each and every one of them in the eye and shook their hands. I acknowledged their decisive win, but I refused to accept it. The experience has motivated my training and team building for the past two years. Every sprint, pullup, bench press, email, and phone call has been done with them in mind. Hatred fuels rivalries.

Last year, things calmed down significantly because they seemed satisfied with their retribution. Also, we had more of our core in place that included Chowder and some other tough guys. Most importantly, we had taken a big competitive step forward, and a close game didn't allow them the opportunity to take selfish penalties. They beat us again, but by the end of the game we were able to identify the players who couldn't contribute to a winning team at the national level. This year, we have upgraded every one of those players with younger, faster, and more talented replacements. We finally have guns for the gunfight.

By the time we get to Tampa, we are more than ready to play, but our game is not until 10:45pm. This gives us time to go to the Post Card Inn on St Pete Beach, which has been the Eagles landing spot for over 20 years. We check into the beachfront hotel that used to be a run-down Travelodge but has been renamed and turned into somewhat of a resort. It has become a familiar, exciting ritual, as has the 50 minute drive back north to the rink. Seeing the USA Hockey tables set up in the main foyer of the Brandon Ice Forum immediately kicks up the butterflies in my stomach. As I register myself and collect the swag for the team, I see familiar faces from other teams, including Famous Joe's. They look jovial and relaxed, as if they fully expect to run over us again tonight.

True to their word all the players who said they will be here gradually filter in. I recognize Hamrlik immediately and introduce myself. Petr is with him and gives me more bad news; he is sick and may not be able to play this game. We're down to 11 skaters, and the game hasn't even started. I remind myself that overcoming adversity is a big part of winning championships and head to the dressing room to do the remaining introductions and game preparations. It's my job to take care of housekeeping, and Bob's is to inspire. I let everyone know what the lines are, and then turn it over. As he does every year he welcomes the new players to the team and talks about the history and tradition of the Eagles logo and his pride in wearing it. If delivered by anyone else, it might come across as melodramatic, but Bob feels it with every fiber of his being. That type of genuine intensity is not only infectious but it also loosens us up.

I chuckle to myself imagining what must be going through Hamrlik's mind, probably something like, *ooh boy, what have I gotten myself into*?

I look around the room, and the expressions tell me that the new guys are either curious, amused, or both. This is pretty much the reaction that I was hoping for, and I feel good as we leave the dressing room for the ice. One of the Joe's players who came at me the hardest two years ago was the captain, who coincidentally played most of his pro career in Greensboro. As the teams move around the ice for warmup, he skates past me and says, "I see you've added a few players."

I give him a wry smile, 'Yeah, a couple."

We exchange sportsmanlike shin pad taps, and go our separate ways knowing that this year is going to be much different. Right from the drop of the puck the pace is quick, and we carry the play. Their goalie has always been one of their best players, and tonight is no different. In the three previous meetings, the North Carolina Eagles have scored a grand total of two goals against him. For most of the first period, he holds them in the game, but we keep pressing. Finally, Jocelyn breaks the scoreless tie and gives us our first ever lead against them. By the time we go to the dressing room for the ice resurfacing between the 2nd and 3rd periods, we have a 2-1 lead.

I know the game is a long way from over, and now Petr, who had started the game, tells me he is too sick to continue. It's concerning, but I also know that right now their goalie is the only reason this game is close. I adjust the lines and we head out for the third to finish the job. We score one more in the third period and grind out the rest of the game for the win. As we shake hands, I sense shock from them more than anything. It feels good to look them in the eyes this time, but I don't celebrate too much. With the round robin tournament format, they can still make the semi-finals, so I fully expect that we will see them again. I will worry about that tomorrow because the beer is on ice and the beach bars await.

I always enjoy the drive from Brandon to St Pete Beach, but tonight as we sail 200 feet in the air over the Sunshine Skyway Bridge with music cranked and the windows down, there's nowhere else I want to be. We know that one more win will get us in the semi-final, and we suspect that we have already beaten our most difficult opponent. Other than this late game, the rest of our times are good - late afternoon or early evening – so we will have our fun every night too. Jimmy B's beach bar is 100 feet from our hotel, and that is where we land again tonight. We get some tables out on the deck overlooking the ocean and have fun talking about the game.

Before long Bob's speech comes up. Chowder loves to needle Bob and tells the group of wives and girlfriends, "Hamrlik's sitting there thinking *this fucking guy is nuts!*" Everyone laughs knowing he is probably right.

When we get back to our room, which Dawn and I are sharing with Bob, he lets us in on his plans for an even bigger pregame speech. He has decided that, when we need it, he will use Rocky's speech to his son in the movie Rocky Balboa. As he plays the clip on his iPhone, he paces back and forth rehearsing what he is going to add to "But it ain't about how hard you hit; it's about how hard you can get hit, and keep moving forward; how much you can take and keep moving forward. That's how winning is done!"

Dawn and I are usually pretty superstitious about assuming wins before they happen, but this time we let Bob get on his roll. These words not only describe how I feel about hockey but also how I've come to learn to deal with life.

As the weekend progresses, it becomes clear that Bob will get the chance to motivate the team again. We defeat Buffalo 10-3 and Chicago 4-2, which, as expected, sets up the rematch with Famous Joe's. The winner will play in the final against whichever team comes out of the other pool. We have had a chance to watch all those teams, and they are clearly much weaker. We know that the winner of this game will win the National Championship. The last real championship – the kind that you have to build towards over several seasons – which I was a part of was in 1991. It took a group of us seven years of working together to finally win the Alberta Provincial

Championships. I consider the coach of those teams, Glenn, to be one of my top two or three mentors. He has spent a great deal of his life shaping and guiding young men, and a lot of it was done as a volunteer.

He often said, “Champions die hard.”

I know very well that it will apply to today’s game. It is clear now that we are the most talented team, but they have proven in the past that they can win. I suspect that they will try being very physical tonight. Bob queues up the Rocky Balboa speech and stands in front of the team. He lets Rocky finish and then talks about how hard we have worked to get to this point. He talks about how much these championships mean, the bonds that you form in these situations, and how they last a lifetime. Unlike his introductory speech two days earlier, there is less amusement. When you take a group of men who have been elite athletes their whole lives and put them in a position to compete for something they value, their passion comes back to them like they are kids again. We feed off Bob and Sly’s words and leave the dressing room with nothing but winning on our mind. This warmup has none of the pleasantries of the first game. Both teams stay on their own side of center ice and focus their preparation.

I notice that they have added a couple of players since the first game, but I am not overly concerned. Petr is feeling better, and Al and Owen arrived on Friday. We have had two games since then to get comfortable with each other, and our lines are gelling. On Friday, I noticed their players watching our other game against Buffalo. A lot of them know each other from pro hockey days, but there is also a program that the tournament organizers put out. It is very easy to look up our guys in hockeydb.com to see where they played, and they have identified our best players. Right from the opening faceoff, we come out with our clean, fast skating style. They are skating with us but, as expected, have added a chippy edge to their play.

In a close hockey game, even if the game is tied and the shots are even, the players can feel which team is getting the edge. One team will find themselves getting a little more tired and feeling a little more pressured with the puck. The trailing team's frustration is triggered more easily, and under those circumstances, players will react in different ways. Some will raise their level, others will disappear, and many start to play dirty. The game is scoreless halfway through the first period, but the momentum is clear. We are pushing Famous Joe's beyond their level, so they turn the game nasty. They come at us in a way that is all too familiar to me. They seem to stay away from Hamrlik, partially out of respect, but mostly because they realize that they are not going to intimidate someone who has gone toe-to-toe with Milan Lucic. They try to come at me again, probably hoping I will take penalties as I did two years ago, but nothing they do phases me. Twenty-five years ago in games just like this, Glenn reminded me, "Fix your eyes on the prize, and be not distracted by the race."

I am squarely focused on the prize, so instead they start in on our offensive players. Jocelyn scored two goals against them in the first game and has been lighting up the tournament ever since. They start taking any liberty they can with him, and their strategy is helped out by the fact that the refs are letting the teams play. Unless it's an obvious penalty, they are looking the other way. This means Joe's hacks, bumps, and even punches us at every opportunity. With the score 0-0 at the end of the first period, Chowder addresses us, "Guys, they're only doing this because they know you're better than them. Just play your game and we'll be fine."

As we skate away from the bench to line up for the second period, Chowder pulls me aside and nods toward Jocelyn, "Watch out for him."

Chowder has seen this strategy many times before, and he knows what we have to do to combat it. My other linemate is Elson, who joined the team a year before I did. We've been playing together ever since, and three minutes into the 2nd period we combine for his most important goal as an Eagle. It's huge, and we feel the anxiety lift. Three minutes later Jocelyn scores, and we know we've got them. We score two more times before the game turns ugly. Every stoppage results in a pushing match. Every time we go into the corner or to the net, we get crosschecked and hit. The refs are losing control of the game and don't seem willing to put a stop to this.

Chowder is generally a very jovial guy, and he doesn't take beer league hockey too seriously. There comes a point, however, when he gets pushed too far, and Joe's is coming dangerously close to that line. As he skates off the ice after yet another shoving match he turns to their bench and yells, "ALL YOU EAST COAST LEAGUE HEROES SETTLE THE FUCK DOWN."

His warning is met with nothing but a chorus of, "FUCK YOU, CHOWDER."

Finally, with about two minutes left in the period, one of our players drives hard to the net, and is punched in the head by one of their East Coast League heroes. There is nothing called on what is an absolutely blatant infraction. On the ensuing faceoff, that player gets the puck and skates down the wing, where he is forced wide and then behind our net. Chowder sees his opportunity, gets a look of pure menace on his face, and steps all of his 300 pound frame into the player as he comes out the other side. The player simultaneously hits Chowder and the end boards, and it's like a yard sale with gloves and sticks all over the ice.

Shaken, he gets up and yells, “WHAT THE FUCK??” The refs finally call a penalty, but this one was worth taking.

As he skates by their bench on the way to the penalty box, Chowder calmly says, “Next time I’ll really hit him.”

Famous Joe’s doesn’t say anything, and they don’t do anything. The message has been delivered: we will take this wherever you want this to go. I don’t think I’ve ever played against a more defeated team than the one we play in the 3rd period. The game ends very quietly 4-0, and I finish with a goal and two assists against a team that I had never registered a point against. I can think of only two more satisfying wins in my entire career, the junior championship and a league championship in Midget. Both of those wins were also against teams who had previously dominated us. I shake Famous Joe’s hands in victory the exact same way I had two years earlier in defeat. When I get to the end of the line, I meet up with their captain and say, “Great run.”

I mean it, but what I keep to myself is, now it’s our turn.

The mood in the dressing room is exuberant but efficient. We want to make it back to the beach for last call because most of us will be leaving directly from the rink after tomorrow’s final. It is a different experience for most of us because, in years past, we have typically been eliminated on Saturday. Cutting into the party time is a sacrifice we will gladly make, but we also don't want to miss out on some well-earned fun.

Two hours later with last call complete, most of the team is still milling about the hotel's outdoor courtyard. We are debating calling it a night when Chowder makes the call, "Everybody get your shit and meet back here!"

I stumble back to my room and get my tequila and meet back at the courtyard five minutes later. By the time I get back, everyone has their shit, which includes a fair amount of weed. It is an understatement to say that Chowder is not a proponent of marijuana legalization. He booms, "I DIDN'T MEAN YOUR SHIT! I MEANT YOUR ALCOHOL."

Undeterred by his subsequent lecturing, everyone else imbibes, which means we are soon ready for bed. Six hours later, even with the extra substance clearing out of my body, it is very easy to wake up. The excitement of a championship game I've been working toward for six years quickly lifts me out of bed and into Bob's SUV. Of all Glenn's expressions, his favorite seemed to be, nothing worthwhile ever comes easily. I can't think of a single accomplishment, accolade or award that I value that doesn't meet that criteria. Getting to this point has been extremely difficult and has helped me in ways that go far beyond hockey. The level of competition requires that I be in shape, so all year I have something for which to train. It has provided an easy way for me to measure if I'm actually moderating or if I'm just lying to myself. I cannot lie to myself out on the ice; I'm either in position or out; I'm either scoring or not. Age has slowed me down slightly, but I refuse to be slowed down by lack of mental toughness.

I have a question to answer: *are drugs and alcohol more important than the other things in my life?* My family, my career, and hockey are all the things I value enough to keep from sliding back into the cycle of addiction. Unfortunately, far too many people are unable to find the things in their life that will keep them from dying.

There is no Bob speech required for the final; we know we will win. The New York team we are playing knows it too, and some of their players don't even bother to show up on time. We score on our first three shifts and win easily 10-1. We don't officially have a captain, so I skate up to accept the banner and trophy from the tournament director. As a part of this ceremony, I also get to present each of my teammates with championship equipment bags and hats. The hats that USA Hockey gives to the winners of its National Championships are white with the USA Hockey logo on the front and "National Champions" on the side. You can purchase USA Hockey branded hats in every color and style, except white. The white hats can only be won.

After the team picture, we retreat to our dressing room to celebrate. Looking around the room I see a group of men brought back to their childhoods. The smiles painted onto their aging faces make them look like little kids. I can imagine what each of them looked like as a ten-year-old when they played the sport for the pure joy of it. Before long the wives and kids join us, and hugs and conversations abound. For a few minutes, I find myself quietly taking it all in and reflecting on the journey to get here. I take off my hat and really inspect it. I contemplate all it represents to me and think to myself, "This, Graeme, is a nice hat."

Two months later, my new dog Emily pulls my hat off the coffee table and chews it. I keep it, but can't really wear it. I guess I have incentive to go win another one.

* * *

It has been exactly three months since Graeme was to be sentenced for his first-degree murder conviction. March 24th did not provide the resolution I had expected. Like everything else in Graeme's case, the defense is successful in delaying the process. They even filed an unsuccessful motion for a mistrial based upon an Internet crime blog post suggesting that at least one juror has been discussing his deliberations online.

Finally, three months and three postponements later, he learns his fate. He gets life in prison with no chance of parole, plus an additional 25 years because a firearm was used in the crime. He has avoided the death penalty, but his life is essentially over. Fittingly, with its Los Angeles Kings glory days long gone, Culver City arena was permanently shut down shortly after Graeme's guilty verdict.

CHAPTER 19 –PSYCHOPATHS

Graeme Bercham steadfastly maintains that he killed his son in self-defense, and filed his appeal in January of 2015. In spite of Graeme's relatively easy conviction, Ryan may not have been the innocent victim he was portrayed to be, and his behavior leading up to the shooting is now at the core of the appeal. It asserts that the judge erred in instructing that the jury could consider all of Graeme's motives, even if Ryan intended to physically harm him and Jasmine.

Starting in the early 1990s, when he was a teenager, Ryan was a regular patient of clinical psychologist Marcus Park. Park then saw Ryan occasionally in the early 2000s and maintained communication right up until the time of his death. Park said there was "no question" Ryan was a violent person, who would not hesitate to inflict physical harm on others if he believed they stood in his way. He was also a known lair with no remorse for making death threats against his parents.

He often told Park that he was going to kill his parents, saying, "I'm going to kill Julia," "I'm going to kill Graeme," and "I'm going to kill Graeme and Julia."

Ryan vowed revenge for things that his parents had done to him; however, any perceived damage was paranoia and delusion based. When Park would ask Ryan if he had a particular plan, he would reply, "No, not yet," so Park never reported the threats. Ryan did admit to Park that he once gave a boyfriend a beating because he felt he deserved it. In addition, family members reported Ryan's violent outbursts. When he was around 20 years old, Ryan beat his brother with a baseball bat, and the attack started while Grant was asleep. Ultimately Park diagnosed Ryan Bercham as a psychopath.

We all encounter people with psychopathic, Machiavellian, and narcissistic personality traits. Together they form what is known as the Dark Triad, and it cannot be avoided. Dark Triad personality traits must have significant evolutionary benefits because they are genetically extremely persistent. It seems clear now that Graeme possesses many of these characteristics, and he successfully procreated. To this day, I have a certain sense of gratitude to the man. I saw what he became and know what he did, but he always treated me well. It is that superficial charm that allows Graeme, and those like him, to fit into civilized society. Until their interests conflict with those around them, they can be hard to identify.

Eventually we all clash with Dark Triads, and I think it's best to fight back hard. My attitude is, why should we give these monsters their way just because they want it? The reason most people avoid these conflicts is they understand how dangerous they are and that they will lash out aggressively when challenged. Their attacks are rife with hypocrisy and they will accuse you of the actions and behaviors that they themselves have perpetrated. Submission is a much easier route but one I disagree with because it allows them to thrive. I think it is incumbent upon everyone with a strong moral compass to fight them. Identify, observe, fight, and remove. It requires determination and strength to withstand their attacks, and I found out just how costly it can be.

* * *

When the Carolina Hurricanes beat the Edmonton Oilers in the 2006 Stanley Cup, Johnathan became a rabid hockey fan. It likely would have happened anyway, but the Cup win intensified his love of hockey. To me, this was more than worth the sacrifice of having my beloved Oilers fall just short of their sixth NHL championship. My son is getting access to hockey largely because of the work that the Hurricanes have done in building the local youth hockey programs. They've even put their name on the championship trophy, and Johnathan wanted nothing more than to win the Canes Cup. Twice, he had been on teams that had their hearts broken in the third period of the championship game. I made it my goal to help him get that first championship, so in 2010 I decided to coach John's team in Raleigh.

Very quickly into our first practice, I realized that even this house league championship was going to be tough to win. I began the season not knowing anyone, so the first practice I was frantically running around trying to manage a bunch excited nine-year-olds. I kept my head above water, made some progress, and afterwards a couple of fathers offered to be assistant coaches. I gladly accepted and we were off and running. By the end of the season, I was spoiled by the parents and the players. Not only did we win the Canes Cup that season, but everyone was amazingly supportive and fun. If all parents behaved the way this group did, youth sports wouldn't have developed a bad reputation.

The good times continued shortly after the season when Sandra decided to move herself and the kids into my house. While my job remained stable, her position at Merrill Lynch was quickly eliminated after the financial meltdown, and things hadn't improved for her since. Her finances finally broke and she realized that the life I was creating in Greensboro would offer the most stability for the kids. It was a temporary arrangement to help her get back on her feet, but it was a defining moment in my life. I had finally come from rock bottom and gotten back what was most important to me.

That fall, I enrolled John in one of the area's hockey programs and applied to coach the team. I assumed, based on my first coaching experience, that it would be another great year. However, I was quickly introduced to the reality of "travel" hockey and the types of individuals that you must deal with in this environment. A good number of these people foolishly believe that their kid is going all the way, and it affects their behavior. This can become a serious problem when you combine these types of parents with a problematic child. Before the season, I had received vague warnings about one particular player and his family. They had been kicked out of their previous hockey organization, but I didn't fully understand why.

I began to see a pattern on road trips. The team would have the opportunity to hang out together at the hotel, which occasionally resulted in a bump or bruise along the way. Other players would typically show concern at the misfortune of one of their teammates, but this kid was the one laughing and pointing his finger in delight. As I observed the family throughout the season, I realized that he had most likely inherited these traits from his mother. Every cheap shot, disrespectful comment, and lie he told was supported with the full backing of the parents.

It's hard to deal with malicious behavior in an eight-year-old because most people don't want to believe it at such a young age. At some point, every one of my players has hit another player with his stick, but in most cases, it's the unavoidable consequence of playing a fast moving sport. It is only when it consistently happens that you can be certain that it is deliberate. The pattern of behavior became very clear, so near the end of the season I decided to dismiss the player from the team. It was a controversial end to a miserable season. I had made enemies of the player's parents, and it was a stark contrast to the triumphant season prior.

That summer, one of my friends who was connected to the mother on Facebook saw a posting of hers saying, "Some people are going to get what they deserve."

Two years later, I was at a rink for Stick & Puck, which is essentially public skate for hockey players. With pucks zipping around and people going in any direction it is controlled chaos. Most people choose to wear full equipment and anyone under eighteen must wear a helmet with a face mask. Kyndal, Johnathan, and I picked a spot along the boards in the center ice area to work on some drills.

Before long, I noticed another kid about their age regularly skating by and attempting to pester them as we were doing the drills. I began to get angry because I thought whatever was driving this behavior was completely unprovoked. We were minding our own business and this kid had taken it upon himself to try to bully them. The next time he did it, I skated over to him and asked him what he wanted. When I got up close, I realized who it was; the dismissed player had changed his appearance since I had seen him last. I almost regretted confronting him because it only intensified his behavior.

When we finished our drills at center ice, my kids and I went separate directions and each did our own puck handling and shooting practice. As I did mine, I noticed that he was watching me. I suspected that he was probably up to something, but I didn't particularly care. I wasn't going to be intimidated by 4'10" tough guy, so I went about my business and headed from the center ice line toward the net to take a shot. I found an open path, and when I got just inside the blue line I wound up for a slap shot. I dropped my head to look at the puck and brought my stick down and through toward the net. As my head came up, I expected to see the puck on course to the net, but it didn't make it. It went about fifteen feet before it hit the boy in the shoulder. In his effort to pester me, he decided that he was going to disrupt my shot. Maybe he thought if he got in my way

I would be irritated but not shoot. Maybe he thought that because he was in full gear he could block it without consequence. Or maybe he just wasn't thinking at all because, even in full gear, getting hit in the shoulder with a puck hurts.

He skated over to the bench, sat down, and started crying. I have hit literally thousands of people with hockey pucks and usually feel bad if someone gets hurt. Had it been anyone else, I would have skated over to apologize and made sure he was taken care of. Given our history, I decided against it. He had done it to himself with his foolishness, it was clear to me that he wasn't severely injured, and I simply considered it to be a self-inflicted spanking he had needed for years. What didn't occur to me was the opportunity for revenge. An effective technique of Dark Triads is that they often seek positions of authority or ingratiate themselves to those in such positions.

His mother was at the rink; when she realized that he had a minor injury and that I had shot the puck, she immediately called 9-1-1. Two cops arrived within minutes and I saw the mother earnestly speaking with them. Soon they summoned me off the ice and began to question me. I told them what had happened and thought that would be the end of it, but in The South many still do not understand even the basics of hockey.

In more traditional hockey markets, they would have asked these individuals why they were wasting valuable police resources with something that happens millions of times every year. Instead, Barney Fife had his partner wait with me while he questioned skaters who witnessed what had happened. The partner explained to me that in order for it to be a crime, I had to have shot the puck with malice. The mother had told Barney about our history, that I never liked her son, and that she was certain that I had done this for some sort of retribution. Some of her friends who were also there told him that I was a real hot head, so Barney was obviously asking people if they thought I hit the boy on purpose. Before long, he returned and informed me that I was free to go but that the case would be held open for further investigation. This meant that no one he had questioned thought I did it on purpose, but more taxpayer resources were going to be wasted on an investigation.

A few days later, I got a call from a detective whose name I initially thought was Coughdrop. He explained that he, *needed to ask me some questions* and that *I needed to come down to the police station to answer them.* I could tell from his smug, overconfident tone that he had every intention of arresting me. There are many reasons that Coughdrop may have decided that this was something to pursue. It could have been his obvious ignorance of hockey and likelihood of being hit by a puck every time you step on the ice. Maybe he is one of the many Dark Triads attracted to the power that comes with a badge, and he identified with the mother. Most likely, he has poor analytical skills and was duped by superficial charm and persuasion.

Even with no formal training in police work, I know enough to understand that if he had enough evidence to arrest me, the responding officers would have done so immediately. I also know, however, that bad or ambitious cops have a long history of railroading people – never speak to one without an attorney present. It is not a matter of *lawyering up*; it is a fundamental right not to have your life ruined by overzealous law enforcement. I'm certain Coughdrop was going to try to coerce a confession from me. I refused to accept that, so I immediately hired a lawyer, who collected statements and evidence on my behalf. When presented with a full picture of the incident, Coughdrop had no choice but to close the investigation and move on to actual crimes. Unfortunately, some damage was done. He had not only inconvenienced me, but he had also emboldened a disrespectful young man, teaching him exactly how to use the police to do your bidding.

I have no regrets about shooting that puck, and it doesn't bother me that the boy's stupidity caused him to get hurt. Regardless of how I feel about the incident after the fact, the fundamental question to be resolved was my intent at the time. My *only* reason for shooting that puck was to practice putting it in the net. As much as Coughdrop may have wanted to manufacture evidence to the contrary, he simply couldn't. This was a relief because, as Graeme Bercham found out, even a partial motive of wanting to hurt someone is grounds for arrest and conviction. The behavior of the victim is almost irrelevant if the perpetrator has a motivation of malice. I observed how easily Danette Myers maneuvered around Ryan's psychological profile and past history of violence because of statute CALCRIM 505, which covers the issue of intent as it pertains to self-defense. During deliberations, the jury needed clarification on the issue.

They asked, "Does the primary reason for the killing have to be for financial gain, or can financial gain be only part of the reason the killing was carried out?"

The court instructed that it needed only be part of the reason, thus setting up the key argument for Graeme's appeal. He is challenging not only that jury instruction but also the CALCRIM 505 statute itself, which states, "The defendant must have believed there was imminent danger of death or great bodily injury to himself or someone else. Defendant's belief must have been reasonable and he must have acted only because of that belief."

In arguing for the allowance of mixed motives, Graeme asserts, "Both the state of the evidence and the jury's questions provide good reason to believe that erroneous instructions on self-defense and the financial gain special circumstance made the difference in this case. Based on a misreading of Penal Code section 198, the instructions told jurors that if they believed appellant killed Ryan in self-defense, they still had to find him guilty of murder unless he acted only from fear. In reality, California law does not, and constitutionally cannot, impose such a requirement on someone who reasonably believes he must kill his assailant to save his own life. And even if self-defense could be limited in this way, the killer would nevertheless lack malice and so the homicide would be voluntary manslaughter rather than murder. While the instructions defined self-defense too narrowly, the jury got an overly-broad definition of the special circumstance. Contrary to the ordinary, accepted meaning of the term 'for financial gain', the jury was allowed to find the allegation true even if appellant would have killed Ryan in self-defense regardless of any financial benefit."

He goes on to claim that the introduction of testimony related to drug use – my testimony – was unduly prejudicial. "The improper admission of evidence of appellant's conduct, motive, and intent was just as damaging as the instructional errors. The prosecution was unable to produce credible evidence that appellant misappropriated money from the estate or that his drug use drove him to kill. It relied instead on testimony that appellant was using cocaine months before the shooting as well as Ryan's accusations that appellant was draining the estate to feed his drug habit and had told him to make a will naming him as beneficiary."

The final Hail Mary is an obscure pre-1872 legislative investigation into the Rule of Lenity. It states that in construing an ambiguous criminal statute, a court should resolve the ambiguity in favor of the defendant. The Due Process Clause, as manifested in the rule of lenity, prohibits an expansive reading of a criminal statute. As it applies to his case, Graeme argues that even if he was partially motivated by the prospect of financial gain, "but for" Ryan Bercham's actions, the shooting would never have taken place. If Graeme legitimately feared for his or Jasmine's life, in that moment, the malice required for first degree murder is irrelevant.

At trial, the defense initially rested without testimony from Graeme. His statements to arresting officers regarding the protection of Jasmine were a key component of his defense; however, the court did not find those statements to be enough evidence to instruct the jury as such. It therefore allowed him to reopen his case and testify, thus giving his self-defense plea, and subsequent appeal, at least some basis in evidence.

Graeme weaved a tale of mental health issues, substance abuse, and violence. He told the court that Ryan's anger had always been off the charts, and he had been treated by mental health professionals since he was five. He had many hospitalizations, during which he made numerous threats to kill his parents. In response to being asked how he would kill his parents, Ryan listed possibilities such as making them overdose on medication or causing a mechanical problem with their car. Ryan claimed he would be able to cover up the murder because he had been diagnosed as a criminal mastermind at age fourteen.

Official records are somewhat contradictory to Graeme's version of Ryan's confinements. He never expressed any immediate intent or gave a specific plan, and followed up by saying he was joking. In the end, all his statements were deemed to be nothing more than empty threats, and doctors concluded Ryan could be discharged in "very good condition."

Graeme further testified that as an adult, Ryan abused methamphetamine, benzodiazepines, and was depressed and suicidal. Hospital records showed Ryan admitted himself to Glendale Memorial Hospital's mental health unit on December 13, 2004 and was discharged on December 24, 2004. He admitted himself again on January 5, 2005, staying until January 18, 2005. According to Ryan's boyfriend Simon Roth and his Alcoholics Anonymous sponsor Paul Smith, Ryan had been sober for two or three years. Neither had witnessed Ryan being violent.

Even with substance abuse issues seemingly behind him, and Marcus Park unwilling to say for certain that Ryan was still violent in 2007, Graeme was able to recount for the court a long history of violent behavior. Ryan acted out toward both Grant and Julia, and she gave up on him after a physical assault in 1991. After that point Ryan was no longer welcome in the family home, but Graeme said he continued to give Ryan money and made sure he had a place to live. He even allowed Ryan to live with him when the couple separated for three years.

Between 2002 and 2005 there were a number of encounters in which Ryan pushed and shoved his father. Ryan would also frequently threaten him, saying "I'm gonna get you. I'm gonna kill you."

Ryan would usually cover himself by relenting and saying, "I'm joking."

Graeme also told the court about violence toward those outside the family. Ryan had told Graeme that while he was living in Montreal, he and a female friend would rob and beat up homosexuals. Ryan later expressed pride about an incident in which he threw a drink in a girl's face at a convenience store. Those stories were never confirmed, but Grant's girlfriend was another person who had accused Ryan of assault. Then in 2005,

Ryan allegedly attacked his middle-aged, Parkinson stricken boyfriend, Michael.

With such a long history of violence, Graeme was not surprised that his relationship with Jasmine Getty was the trigger for sending Ryan's anger into a dangerous spiral. He testified that Ryan would speak poorly of Jasmine on an almost daily basis and threatened to physically remove her from the Larchmont house.

"I want your nigger crack whore out of my mom's house, out of my mom's bed, not prancing around in front of my mom's ashes," he would say.

Ryan allegedly told Graeme that sometime in late February he snuck into the house and, while Jasmine was sleeping, he grabbed her by the hair. He then pulled her out of the house and said, "Get the hell out of my mother's house. This is strike one. Next time is strike two."

Graeme and Ryan met at the bank on the morning of March 2, and they discussed signing loan papers so that Ryan could have money from the estate. When Graeme returned home from the bank he said he heard yelling and screaming. He went inside and saw Ryan holding a shortened hockey stick like a billy club and pounding it on the door to the master bedroom. The door was dead-bolted and Jasmine was behind it yelling and screaming. Ryan was on the other side screaming back.

He turned to Graeme and said, “This is strike two. The next time I come back will be strike three. Get this nigger crack whore out of my house, or I’m coming back and I’m going to take her out.”

Ryan then made a final threat before leaving. He turned to the locked door, which stood between him and Jasmine, and yelled, “The next strike you’ll get the fuck out of here if I have to take you out.”

Graeme testified that Ryan’s threats continued over the phone throughout the day. Ryan called at some point during the day and said “strike three” was coming. He also called to say he was coming over to physically remove Jasmine from the house. When Ryan returned later that afternoon he was apparently also angry because Grant pawned his mother’s ring and Graeme had not informed him. He presented Graeme with a pawn ticket and the two got into a yelling match.

Ryan then began pounding on the bedroom door with a hockey stick, yelling, “You fucking nigger crack whore, get the fuck out of this house.”

Graeme asked Ryan, “What the hell are you doing?”

Ryan replied, “If you don’t get that fucking nigger out of here, I’m going to hit her.”

Ryan threw the hockey stick at Graeme but missed. Before walking out the door he said, “This is strike three.”

Graeme armed himself because he wanted to use the gun to scare Ryan but had not chambered a round. When Ryan reentered the house with a mallet, he came in quick, angry, and loud. Graeme was in fear for himself and his girlfriend. Based on what had happened earlier, he was certain Ryan had returned to attack her. When Ryan saw the gun, he became enraged and raised the mallet. Graeme did not know what Ryan was holding, so when Ryan raised his weapon Graeme responded in kind. Ryan then went toward the kitchen before turning to hit Graeme, at which point Graeme fired. He did not remember firing any warning shots, but he did not aim anywhere that would seriously hurt Ryan. Graeme believed the first two rounds hit him but wasn't sure where and just hoped that it would cause him to leave.

He testified that instead of leaving, Ryan retreated to the kitchen and assumed a baseball batter's position, ready to knock his head off. Graeme said he attempted to fire but the gun malfunctioned. He got the gun working before Ryan was able to strike him and fired the fatal shots.

There was no forensic evidence presented by the prosecution to definitively refute Graeme's version of the confrontation. It could not be determined in what order Ryan's wounds were sustained, except that the instantly fatal wound likely would have occurred last. Ryan's body did not have any soot or stippling on it, which suggests he was shot from at least two or three feet away. Further, if Ryan had been shot while on the floor, there could have been "pseudo stippling." No such pseudo stippling was identified. One complicating factor for Graeme was how Ryan could have been found with the mallet still in his hand. A gunshot wound probably would have caused Ryan to drop the mallet; however, about 20% of people who are found dead after shooting themselves in the head still have a gun in their hand.

While forensic evidence didn't hurt Graeme's version of events, it could not help prove anything about his intent. As was the case with his trial, the appeal will hinge on whether or not people believe him. It is a longshot at best.

CHAPTER 20 – SON

"How did you get here son?" My father's words have never left me.

I've been here before but never thought I would be back. Sitting on a bench, I look around the small, sterile room with nothing to do but wait. I'm tired. I have been in this hospital for almost twelve hours, and I won't be leaving anytime soon. My anxiety is quite high, but I am doing what I can to manage it because everything else is beyond my control. There's nothing to do but stare down at my scrubs and ponder how I got here. I suppose I could thank that douche bag cop, Coughdrop, because he's the one responsible for this. In fact, I don't thank him – I would love to get him out on the ice and go a round or two with him – but he was certainly a significant catalyst for this.

When I saw the way that Dawn had my back while I was being investigated for assault, I knew I would never find anyone more committed to me. She got on the phone and started making calls, mining her hockey network. It became evident that she knows everyone from every walk of life. She contacted every cop she knows, eventually managing to get me a copy of the police report. My attorney wound up being a police recommendation, and in the two weeks it took to clear my name and reputation, she had earned my loyalty. Most importantly, I know that everything she did for me was done without an ulterior motive. We have been together for over six years now, and it's been obvious for the last four years there is only one thing she really wants from me.

After about ten minutes, the doctor enters, "Alright Daddy, how are you doing?"

"I'm fine. I went through all this with my twins, although that was fifteen years ago."

"So, you know the drill. OK, well they're just getting Mommy prepped. As soon as they're ready we'll come and get you and get started."

She leaves me alone again with my thoughts. It's impossible for me not to think back to the last time I was a part of a delivery. Unlike today, we knew going in that it would have to be a C-section because of the positioning of the twins, but that didn't make the process any easier. It was a tough pregnancy right up to the end, and when they came out Johnathan was quite purple. It took what seemed like at least a minute for them to get his breathing started, and I'll never get those images out of my mind. I can't imagine my life without him or his sister.

That was a much riskier pregnancy; nevertheless, today has been exhausting. They tried for about eight hours to induce labor, but it just wasn't happening. Now, there is some sort of problem with Hayden's heart rate, so the only option is another C-section. I am not panicking, but I will be devastated if something goes wrong.

Dawn opted for the epidural earlier in the day, so it speeds up the pre-op process significantly. Within minutes, the nurse comes for me, and we walk into the operating room. I can sense Dawn's anxiety, and when she looks at me I see in her eyes a vulnerability that she never shows. It is my turn to provide the strength and reassurance she will need to get through a difficult moment. I position myself so that I am safely behind the curtain and cannot see any reflections of the impending cutting, grinding, tugging and burning.

Once I'm seated, they waste no time getting started. I listen intently for any signs of trouble, but everything seems to go smoothly. It takes longer than I remember, and I can't picture what they are doing over there. *Just pull the kid out; what's so hard?*

Finally, the doctor exclaims, "Wow! He's a big one."

The nurse brings Hayden around from behind the curtain for a brief family introduction, then takes me into an adjacent room to cut the umbilical cord. While I am going through the process,

I inspect my new son. Fingers, toes, everything seems to be in perfect order. He is, in fact, a big one and also has a set of lungs on him.

Later, Hayden's half-siblings come to our hospital for some pictures and family time. Dawn is a great step-mom and will be an even better mom. It is not how I envisioned my family twenty years ago, but getting past our idealistic views of what we expect for our lives is big part of growing up. I'm thrilled with the family we've created.

* * *

Upon receiving his life sentence plus twenty-five years, Graeme was sent to Wasco State Prison – Inmate Reception. At Wasco, prisoners are evaluated for such things as criminal records, life history, mental health, and medical issues. They are given a custody score, which determines their assignment to one of California's 34 state prisons. Based on his data, Graeme was assigned to Mule Creek State Prison, about twenty miles southeast of Sacramento. He arrived on July 10, 2014, where he remains to this day. It is there that he receives news that the California Court of Appeal has affirmed his conviction. They rejected not only his claim of self-defense but also every legal argument put forth in his appeal.

The appeals court was able to deny every aspect of Graeme's legal challenge to CALCRIM 505 by noting that the jury found him guilty of first-degree murder. His arguments relied on the assumption that the jury's question about mixed-motive as it related to special circumstances meant that they believed self-defense to be among his motives. The court pointed out, however, that the jury had been instructed to find Graeme guilty of first-degree murder only if he acted "willfully, deliberately, and with premeditation." It follows that they completely rejected his three strikes story; otherwise, his actions would have fallen short of meeting those three criteria. The logical conclusion is that the jury was not factoring in self-defense versus financial gain. Rather, the jury was considering other motives such as hatred or the desire to get Ryan out of the way. There are many possibilities but none that help Graeme.

It seems clear that nobody is ever going to believe that Graeme was legitimately in fear for his safety. He was always in far more danger from the crackheads he was spending time with, but that didn't seem to bother him. What bothered him was when anyone questioned his crazed attachment to Jasmine. I remember the stunned, possessive look he had on his face when I suggested that he take a baseball bat to Jasmine's head. I had no idea that his son had been making similar comments that ultimately led to his death.

The appeals court also rejected the argument related to the overly prejudicial nature of his spending habits and drug abuse. It is a relief to know that I didn't fly across the country, only to have my testimony result in his conviction being overturned. The court did agree that my information was prejudicial to his case but observed that any evidence proving guilt is by nature prejudicial. The type of evidence that cannot be admitted is that which tends to evoke an emotional bias against the defendant as an individual but has very little effect on the issues. Graeme's bad behavior was very relevant but would bias the jury no more than Ryan's documented substance abuse.

There is no doubt Graeme deserves to be in prison, but I do think there were problems with the prosecution case that both the jury and appeals court missed. The verdict of first-degree murder requires that Graeme acted with premeditation. The prosecution presented evidence that Graeme had instructed Ryan to draw up a will. If that was really a part of an elaborate plan, he would have conceived a much more believable threat than having a mallet swung at him. He had guns all over the house and could have easily suggested that Ryan purchase a gun as well. The mallet was too farfetched to have been anything other than improvised. Many other types of weapons would have made more sense. It just so happened that the mallet was available to Graeme in the short amount of time he had to come up with a story.

There was also the matter of the crime scene and Graeme's injuries. Trying to clean up with bleach was a panic move and unnecessary if you've got a properly staged scene. Moreover, Graeme would not have set himself up to engage in a physical battle with Ryan, who was much younger, bigger, and likely stronger. The evidence showed that Ryan was able to deliver a significant blow to Graeme's head, which easily could have resulted in a different outcome to the deadly confrontation. No, Graeme was too smart to devise a plan that required last minute cleaning and put him in physical jeopardy.

What I believe is that Ryan and Graeme began arguing about the estate. Ryan told him he was taking control and kicking him out. The mixture of cocaine use, the asset freeze, and Ryan's threats and/or derogatory comments towards Jasmine finally sent Graeme into a murderous rage. They fought, Graeme drew his weapon, started firing, and chased Ryan through the house. When he caught up to his son, he put two bullets into his head, thus committing second-degree murder.

Whether it was premeditated or not, he will deservedly spend the rest of his life in jail. Why would any father choose a drug addicted whore over his child? It is unfathomable, indefensible, and unforgivable. In the end, we'll never know for sure if

Graeme was an evil psychopath executing his son for money or a stupid, irrational fool whose weaknesses brought him down forever.

There is only one person who could answer this question, but the prosecutor's investigators couldn't find her to testify. Even if they had, you probably can't believe anything that comes out of her mouth. She is a despicable animal who should pay a severe price for her role in this, but sometimes Clyde takes the fall so Bonny can walk. Graeme will never again see the light of day, and she is gone baby gone, likely hiding in plain sight.

CHAPTER 21 – DANGEROUS GAME

I imagine it goes something like this.

* * *

As she looks around the small, dingy apartment, the anger builds. It's been two years since she had to rabbit, and there's no end in sight. Laying low is bad enough, but it's even worse when you were living large off some clueless, old cracker. Then he had to go and fuck the shit all up, and she is the one suffering because that pathetic loser couldn't keep it together. The money his lawyer gave her to get gone is long spent, and for all she knows they are planning on dragging things out another ten years. She hasn't bothered to call for an update in six months, but she knows the answer anyway - stay gone. The cops still want her.

Now, she's getting desperate because the only money coming in is from the occasional trick, which isn't exactly easy when you can't risk getting bopped. She storms over to the closet, throws open the doors, and feels the anger change to a blind rage. HE FUCKED UP EVERYTHING. She had him on the hook so good she could have bled his shit for another five years. She wishes she could go back and shoot some motherfuckers herself.

His peeps wanted to say she was the cause of it all. She has two words for them: FUCK and YOU.

"That shit ain't on me," she screams in her mind, "he did it. That was all him."

There is nothing in the closet to calm her down. It's not that it's empty, far from it, but it's mostly old ghetto shit from before the white boy. Not only did she lose everything that was in the house when the cops came, but her shopping has also been nonexistent ever since. A little bit of panic and a lot of self-pity filter in to her mind. She needs another sugar daddy paying for shit real quick, and she goddammed deserves it. Her asshole father cut her off, so some other chump has to pay.

She has grudgingly accepted that she can't go back but at least she knows her type of people are everywhere. She ain't happy about it, but with a little bit of working it she has gradually found the dealers, hookers, and a couple regular johns that will get her by. She is intent on getting another whale on the hook, and she has heard some of her new girls talking about one. There is no more time to wait, so she is going after him tonight. Leaving nothing to chance, she used her last $1500 on a pair of

Balmain Jeans and Louis Vuitton shoes. She puts them on, along with a very low cut Versace blouse and her Cartier watch, the only decent thing her father ever gave her. The final touch is a little Chanel behind her ears, so when she leans in real close he'll know very clearly that he is in.

It all means she won't be paying for any drinks, but booze won't be enough to calm her nerves with so much on the line. Her new dealer is fat and ugly, and that makes him easy to manipulate - he gave her some great shit after she fucked him real good. This is how it's going to have to be for now, so she will make what he gave her last. Just a small bump to get her going and then a little Demerol to smooth it out. She gets the Gucci bag that the pathetic, old fuck bought her, then takes out the tiny spoon and small vial filled with white powder. After snorting a little up each nostril, she finds her pills. She takes two and sits for a couple minutes, waiting for the comfort and, a minute later, elation.

Now feeling optimistic, she walks outside, climbs into her Toyota, and sits down on the tattered cloth driver seat. She puts the key into the ignition and turns it over. Fifteen seconds of cranking, and it finally starts. She knows it's not going to last much longer, but it only has to get her there because she won't be leaving alone. If it has to be a trick, so be it, but hopefully she'll find a more permanent *arrangement*.

For a few moments, she walks around the bar like she owns the place. Observing. Smiling. Planning. Finally, she thinks she sees him across the bar. He fits the description: late 50s, no wedding ring, and a nicely tailored old white boy sport coat. Even if it's not the one the girls have been talking about, he'll do.

The hunt begins with an intent gaze and the occasional hair flip. His present conversation with the bartender keeps him from noticing, so she starts moving closer to him with a slightly exaggerated hip swing. Several minutes later, he is still enjoying the sound of his own voice, and she is getting frustrated.

"Do I have to go over there and hit him across the head?"

She has to casually dance her way within ten feet of him to finally get his attention. He gives her an enthusiastic smile before instinctively averting his eyes. Bingo. She likes the ones with a little insecurity. She stalks over to him, gently brushing her chest against his back as she circles around behind him. She slides into the open stool next to him and swivels toward him.

"Hi," she purrs.

Trying his best to be smooth, he responds with, "How are you pretty lady?"

"Never better," she lies.

The bartender approaches, "Can I get you a drink?"

Pretending that she is still making up her mind, she coyly says, "I guess I'll have a Ciroc and Red Bull."

"Put this on my tab," he eagerly volunteers, and she knows she's got him.

"Thanks, honey. What's your name?" She is almost certain she knows the answer.

"I'm Graeme," he smiles as he reaches out his hand.

She offers him a dainty fingertip handshake, which belies her true intent. She plans to reach her hand into his chest, pull out his heart, and watch him bleed out. When she's done with him, she will find another one just like the other one before.

She will never stop; people like her never stop. She can't, at least not until a beast at bay finally puts a bullet through *her* brain.

Made in the USA
Columbia, SC
13 January 2018